AMELIA EARHART

BLYTHE RANDOLPH

AMELIA EARHART

Franklin Watts / 1987
New York / London / Toronto / Sydney
An Impact Biography

Maps by Vantage Art

Photographs courtesy of:
UPI/Bettmann Newsphotos: frontispiece, pp. 33 (top), 40, 70, 73;
The Schlesinger Library, Radcliffe College: pp. 14, 19, 27, 38, 66;
The Smithsonian Institution: pp. 24, 33 (bottom); Seaver Center for
Western History Research, Natural History Museum of Los
Angeles County: pp. 48, 82, 86, 100, 103; AP/Wide World: p. 52;
The Bettmann Archive: pp. 66 (inset), 74; Office of
Public Information, Lockheed-California Company,
Burbank, CA: pp. 89, 92.

Library of Congress Cataloging-in-Publication Data

Randolph, Blythe,
Amelia Earhart.

(An Impact biography)
Bibliography: p.
Includes index.
Summary: The life and career of the famous aviator,
from her girlhood in Kansas, through her successes
breaking aviation records and her increasing fame, to
her mysterious disappearance.
1. Earhart, Amelia, 1897–1937—Juvenile literature.
2. Air pilots—Biography—Juvenile literature.
[1. Earhart, Amelia, 1897–1937.   2. Air pilots]
I. Title.
TL540.E3R36   1987   629.13'092'4   [B]   [92]   86-26651
ISBN 0-531-10331-5

CONTENTS

for my mother

Please know that I am
quite aware of the hazards.
I want to do it because
I want to do it.
Women must try to do
things as men have tried.
When they fail, their
failure must be but a
challenge to others.

Amelia Earhart
Last Flight

THE MYSTERY

1

It was Friday, November 24, 1961. News headlines, however, covered a story that had begun twenty-four years before:

DISCOVERY REVIVES EARHART MYSTERY

NEW EARHART CLUE FOUND IN ISLE GRAVE

BODY FLOWN HERE . . . AMELIA EARHART'S?

AMELIA EARHART BONES FOUND IN ISLE GRAVE?

MYSTERY BONES RENEW AMELIA EARHART CASE

This was the lead story for almost every newspaper, wire service, radio station, and television network in the United States. Almost a quarter century after flier Amelia Earhart's plane had disappeared over the Pacific on the last leg of her round-the-world flight, bones believed to be hers and her copilot's had been excavated on Saipan and were winging their way toward San Francisco to be examined by an archaeological expert. When the bones arrived at San Francisco International Airport, over a thousand people of all ages were waiting. Some had been present when Earhart had taken off on her last flight in 1937. Others, far too young to have been alive in 1937, showed just as keen an interest in the proceedings.

The recovery of the bones was a result of the work of Fred Goerner, a CBS radio broadcaster in San Francisco. Goerner had become interested in the Amelia Earhart story after hearing rumors that Earhart and her copilot, Fred Noonan, had flown off course and made an emergency landing in the Japanese-held Marshall Islands. According to this theory, they had been captured by the Japanese and taken to Saipan, where they had been executed or died in captivity. The story fueled an intense investigation by Goerner in both the United States and the South Pacific, which culminated in the finding of the bones in a Saipan cemetery. Even after the bones were found to be those of Saipan natives and not of the American fliers, Goerner continued his investigation for years, traveling thousands of miles and interviewing hundreds of people in an extraordinary search to discover the truth about the disappearance.

Goerner was, and is, not alone in his desire to know what really happened to Amelia Earhart. Many others have conducted exhaustive research into the same question, and both the American public and the world have shown enormous interest in the disappearance. Over the years, many theories have been offered: that Amelia was on a spy mission authorized by President Franklin Roosevelt and was captured; that she purposely dove her plane into the Pacific; that she was captured by the Japanese and forced to broadcast to American GIs as "Tokyo Rose" during World War II; and that she still lives on an island in the South Pacific with a native fisherman. Even today, fifty years after her disappearance, the very mention of her name is enough to raise conjecture—and stir the imagination.

KANSAS CHILDHOOD

2

When the passage of the Kansas–Nebraska Bill in 1854 divided these two territories, abolitionists formed the Emigrant Aid Company to aid immigration into Kansas and make it a free state. Among those who settled there was a young man named Alfred Gideon Otis. A lawyer who had been born in New York State, Otis was the first man to graduate with honors from the law school of the University of Michigan. One of his ancestors was James Otis, who had proposed the Stamp Act Congress in 1765 and thereby had helped to begin the American Revolution.

Alfred traveled by overland stage from Kalamazoo, Michigan, to Chicago. He then went by flatboat to St. Louis and up the Missouri River to settle in Atchison, Kansas. He and several friends staked claims to the best land and helped to build the area into a thriving railroad town. In addition to becoming a judge, Alfred was named president of the Atchison Savings Bank and became quite wealthy thanks to wise land speculation. He would become Amelia Earhart's grandfather.

Alfred brought his wife, Quaker-born Amelia Harres of Philadelphia, west by train and steamer in 1862 and built a large, handsome brick-and-frame house for his family on a bluff called Quality Hill, which overlooked a great bend in the Missouri River. Mrs. Otis had many servants, appropriate to her station as the wife of one of Atchison's most prominent citizens.

Life in the early days of their marriage, however, was anything but easy for the gentle Philadelphia girl. Atchison was still a frontier town. "Great piles of buffalo bones lined the newly built railroad tracks when she came," Amelia Earhart would later write of her grandmother, "and Indians in blankets were always to be seen in the town. I remember her telling me of their crowding about her when, as a young housewife, she went to market. They lifted the lid of her basket and peered within, and felt the fabric of her dress, until she was quite terrified, mistaking their native curiosity for some kind of sinister threats [*sic*]."

Despite these pioneer surroundings, Judge and Mrs. Otis made a proper life for their eight children that was composed of afternoon teas, neighborly calls, private schooling for the children, books, music, and observance of what was considered socially correct. Their fourth child, Amy, would become Amelia Earhart's mother.

Amy was a born leader among the young people of Atchison in the 1880s. She was an intelligent and cultured young woman, interested in books, art, music, and politics. She was also a good horsewoman and a popular dancer.

When she was sixteen, she suffered an attack of typhoid fever, and her hearing was affected. Later, when she was nineteen and preparing to enter Vassar, she contracted diphtheria. After a slow recovery, she decided not to enter college. Instead she accompanied her father on his business trips into the territories of Utah, Oklahoma, and Colorado. During one of these trips, she became the first woman to climb the last quarter mile to the top of Pikes Peak.

On the night of her presentation to Atchison society in 1890, her brother Mark introduced her to his college roommate, Edwin Stanton Earhart, who was attending law school at the University of Kansas. The young couple fell in love almost immediately.

Edwin's family was very different from the Otis family. Edwin's father, the Reverend David Earhart, was an Evangelical Lutheran missionary who rode 50 miles (80 km) on horseback each Sunday to preach to both Indians and settlers, taught school during the week, and worked a small farm. He was barely able to support his wife and twelve children. Dr. Earhart had hoped that his son would follow him into the ministry, but after graduating from Thiel College in Pennsylvania, Edwin decided on law. He worked his way through law school at the University of Kansas by tutoring his classmates, tending furnaces, and even shining shoes.

Stern Judge Otis was not impressed by his daughter's choice of a suitor. He could see that the young man had some good traits—immense personal charm, intelligence, and love of culture—but also that he lacked the determination to be a success in his chosen career. He made the couple wait five years to marry, insisting that Edwin be earning at least $50 a month. After graduating in 1894, Edwin obtained work as a claims settler for the railroad for exactly that salary. The couple finally married in 1895, and they moved to Kansas City to live in a house bought and furnished by the bride's father.

The move was a painful one for Amy. Accustomed to being surrounded by family and friends, she frequently lacked even the company of her husband, who was often away on business. She began to visit her parents with increasing frequency. When she became pregnant again after her first child was stillborn, her parents insisted that she stay with them until after the birth. So Amelia Mary Earhart was born in her grandparents' home in Atchison on July 24, 1897.

Amy would later write that Amelia was an "eight and a half pounder whose weight was not due to excess fat

Amelia at age 6

because her bones were small and nicely covered. She was already tall with a beautifully shaped head and nice hands, a real water color baby with the bluest of blue eyes, rosy cheeks and red lips. . . ."

In Amelia's early years, money was always a problem for the Earharts. Edwin's work also necessitated that he do a great deal of traveling, and Amy decided that she should travel with him. Therefore, Amelia spent winters with her rich grandparents in Atchison and more modest summers with her parents in Kansas City. She attended the private and proper College Preparatory School in Atchison, but was less proper in after-school hours. Amelia and her younger sister Muriel, or "Pidge," wore bloomers, played football, shot a .22-caliber rifle, and rode boys' sleds. The girls' enlightened and unconventional parents believed that they would benefit from such experiences, but their grandmother was horrified. Amelia later wrote in her book *The Fun of It* (1932):

I know that I worried my grandmother considerably by running home from school and jumping over the fence which surrounded her house. "You don't realize," she said to me one day, "that when I was a small girl I did nothing more strenuous than roll my hoop in the public square." I felt extremely unladylike and went around by the gate for several days in succession. Probably if I'd been a boy, such a shortcut would have been entirely natural. I am not suggesting that girls jump out of their cribs and begin training, but only that the pleasure from exercise might be enhanced if they knew how to do correctly all the things they can do without injuring themselves or giving a shock to their elders. Of course, I admit some elders have to be shocked for everybody's good now and then.

Despite their different opinions as to what constituted ladylike behavior, Amelia and her grandmother loved each other deeply. It was from her grandmother that Amelia first learned the Quaker ideals of pacifism and social service that she would support intensely all her life.

Her grandfather was a different kind of influence. Disgusted with Amelia's father and the poor provision he believed Edwin was making for his family, the judge nevertheless adored his brave and intelligent granddaughter, and in her love of adventure she seemed to have inherited his pioneering spirit. She had also inherited another of his qualities. Despite her idealism Amelia was, throughout her life, a thoroughly practical person in financial matters.

Several of Amelia's and Muriel's early escapades were particularly memorable. Angered by the cruelty to horses described in the children's novel *Black Beauty*, the girls began to watch for horse owners who kept tight checkreins on their horses. If the owners ignored their pleas for humanity, nine-year-old Amelia and six-year-old Pidge simply unchecked the horses themselves. One day the milkman complained because Amelia had unchecked his horse. To the girls' surprise, although their mother lectured them on minding their own business, she did not punish them. Amy even suggested gently to the milkman that his horse might perform better if he were allowed to lower his head.

On another occasion, after a visit to the 1904 St. Louis Fair, Amelia and Pidge fashioned a "rolly coaster" for themselves. The track ran from the roof of the family toolshed, and unfortunately Amelia, who was the first one to try their invention, was unceremoniously dumped from the cart when it ran off the trestle. Adults came running and later dismantled the hazardous contraption while the girls were asleep.

Despite such episodes, these were happy days. "Throughout the grade school period, which was mostly spent in Atchison," Amelia wrote in *The Fun of It*, "I remember having a very good time. There were regular games and school and mudball fights, picnics, and exploring raids up and down the bluffs of the Missouri River. The few sandstone caves in that part of the country added so much to our fervor that exploring became a rage."

All was not action, however. Both girls read before they were five, and Amelia's vivid imagination warmed to the novels of Victor Hugo, Alexandre Dumas (both father and son), Charles Dickens, and Oliver Optic's success stories for boys. She read these with one regret, however: girls or women were never the focus of the action. In an essay she was later to write as an adult, she commented:

There are no heroines following the shining paths of romantic adventure, as do the heroes of boys' books. For instance, who ever heard of a girl—a pleasant one—shipping on an oil tanker, say, finding the crew about to mutiny and saving the captain's life (while quelling the mutiny) with a well-aimed disabling pistol shot at the leader of the gang! No, goings-on of this sort are left to the masculine characters, to be lived over joyously by the boy readers. Of course girls have been reading the so-called "boys' books" ever since there were such. But consider what it means to do so. Instead of closing the covers with shining eyes and the happy thought, "That might happen to me someday!" the girl, turning the final page, can only sigh regretfully, "Oh, dear, that can never happen to me—because I'm not a boy!" . . . Of course before girls' books such as I have hinted at can be written, women must have accomplished enough to supply the material.

She herself already showed signs of being the kind of person to become involved in adventure. Years later one of her cousins was asked what Amelia was like as a child and replied, "All I knew was that Amelia was more fun to play with than anyone else—I admired her ability, stood in awe of her information and intelligence, adored her imagination, and loved her for herself—and it held true always."

In 1907, when Amelia was ten, her father was transferred to Des Moines, Iowa, where he was put on salary in the claims department of the Rock Island Railroad, and in 1908 Amelia and Pidge joined their father and mother in their new home. Although money was still scarce, life was generally good for the children. Their father advanced in his new job, yet always seemed to have time to read or tell stories to the girls and to play Indian wars with them and neighboring children on Saturday afternoons. He still traveled in his new job and occasionally took his family along on trips as far away as California. Mrs. Earhart would request school assignments in advance for the girls so they would not fall behind in their schoolwork. Several pleasant summers were spent by the Earharts on Lake Okabena in Worthington, Minnesota, where the family rode horses, milked cows, fished, played tennis, and, in the evenings, danced.

It was during this period in Des Moines that Amelia had her first look at an "aeroplane." Her father took the family to the Iowa State Fair in 1908 and to the flying field at the fairground edge, where he tried to interest Amelia, eleven, and Muriel, eight, in a biplane. Amelia took one look at the plane making an ungainly leap into the air and promptly asked if they could go back to the merry-go-round.

For several years, everything seemed to go well for the Earhart family. Then, unfortunately, Edwin became bored with his job. Something of a dreamer, he was always developing "get rich" schemes that always failed and angered the more practical Amy. Once he even wasted their tax money on a trip to Washington to patent an already patented invention. To make matters worse, he began to drink.

By 1910 "Dad's sickness" had begun to pull the family apart. Two or three times a week Edwin would come home swaying and talking erratically, and his work began to suffer. To save his job, he was persuaded by his boss and Amy to take "the cure" at the Keeley Institute, where he was given a drug that made him violently ill if he drank alcohol. After he came home, he stayed sober for a time as he waited for the Rock Island Railroad to reinstate him.

Unfortunately, around this time, Mrs. Otis died and left a will in which Amy's share of the estate was to be held

Amelia (left), Muriel, the girls' father, Edwin, and a porter on a railroad car in the Atchison railroad yards, 1911

in trust for twenty years or until Edwin Earhart died. Mrs. Otis had been afraid that Edwin would drink Amy's inheritance away. Edwin considered the will an insult and was so depressed by it that he began drinking again. The Rock Island Railroad, hearing of this, refused to reinstate him. Finally in 1913 he got a job as a freight clerk with the Great Northern Railway in St. Paul, Minnesota. The family moved there and Amelia, sixteen, entered Central High as a junior. Her special interests at the time were math and physics, while Muriel leaned more toward English literature.

Amelia was not, socially speaking, very popular in high school. Tall, lean, and freckled, she considered herself physically unattractive. This was a feeling she would never completely outgrow, but she was philosophical about it: "I don't think that boys particularly cared for me," she later wrote, "but I can't remember being very sad about the situation. Probably I didn't get so much exercise at dancing as I should have liked, because of having only one or two faithful partners."

Although Edwin managed to hold on to his low-paying job as a freight clerk, the financial and emotional strain increased tensions within the family. There was also at least one threat of physical violence: Edwin caught Amelia pouring whiskey down the drain and raised his fist but was prevented from harming her by Amy. On another occasion Edwin promised to escort the two girls to a dance at their church. That evening he came home late and in no condition to go. Muriel ran upstairs crying, but Amelia was stoic, which was to be her reaction to all of the problems created by her father's illness.

The family left St. Paul when Edwin was promised a new job in Springfield, Missouri. When they arrived in Springfield, however, they found that the man Edwin was supposed to replace had decided not to retire, so there was no job waiting. It was the last straw. Edwin and Amy decided to separate. Family friends from Des Moines had recently moved to Chicago, and they invited Mrs. Earhart and the girls to move in with them. Edwin decided to go back to Kansas City to live with his sister and her family and try to open a law office there.

Having already attended five high schools, Amelia was determined to make the most of her last one and get decent training in scientific subjects. She refused to go to the nearest high school and chose one farther away that offered better courses in chemistry and physics. Her interests, however, were not limited to science. In her senior year, she became involved in a student movement to have the English teacher, who seemed to her unfit, removed. When the effort failed, Amelia requested and received permission to spend that class period in the library, where she read four times the number of required books for the English course. The caption under her picture in the yearbook was "the girl in brown, who walks alone." When her classmates received their diplomas in June of 1916, she did not even bother to attend the ceremony; she would later receive her diploma from the mayor of Chicago.

The effect of Amelia's early years was profound and lasting. From her pioneering and prosperous grandfather, she gained a sense of both adventure and business. Her Quaker grandmother gave her the ideal of pacifism she would later support. From her father she developed a vivid imagination and a sense of romance. This was tempered by the practicality she had seen lacking in him and present in her mother. The periods of financial and emotional strain suffered as a result of her parents' difficulties and their frequent absences led to the formation of an emotionally independent girl, who had an intense fantasy life, a love for adventure, a strongly protective urge toward her mother and sister, an intense pacifism and idealism, a highly competitive edge, and a discomfort with what society believed should be a woman's role. These traits show up again and again as one looks at her unconventional girlhood and would be much reflected in her later life.

COMING OF AGE

3

The summer after Amelia graduated from high school, the family received good news from Edwin Earhart. He had stopped drinking and was successfully practicing law in Kansas City, so Mrs. Earhart and the girls moved there to be with him. At the same time, Amy Earhart had learned that the inheritance from her parents had been mishandled by her brother while held in trust for her. Persuaded by Edwin to break the trust, she used part of the money to send Amelia to college in the fall of 1916.

The school chosen was the Ogontz School, a small, liberal arts college for women located in the wooded hills a short distance from Philadelphia. It was an expensive school for its day, with tuition, room, and board coming to $600 a semester. Most of the students were from upper-middle-class families and were mainly interested in finding future husbands. The school, however, was a good one. It was well endowed, with a good art gallery and a lecture series with invited speakers, and the headmistress, Abby Sutherland, made a great impression on Amelia. In a letter to her mother Amelia wrote: "She is a very brilliant woman, very impressive as she is taller than I and large . . . she has had many chances of matrimony because she is brilliant but she passes them all by. She has read very widely and has very good ideas about lots of things. . . ." In addition to classes, the young women were taken frequently into Philadelphia for concerts and operas, which Amelia thoroughly enjoyed. She quickly gained "a reputation for brains," and Sutherland later wrote that Amelia "was always pushing into unknown seas in her reading. The look in her straightforward, eager eyes was most fascinating in those days. Her most characteristic charm was her poise, her reserve, her curiosity." Lanky and long-legged, liking basketball and hockey, she cared little for her appearance, and Sutherland remarked that "she helped very much to impress the overindulged girls with the beauty and comfort of simple dressing."

Still a nonconformist, Amelia thoroughly enjoyed the secret sorority she was invited to join until she realized that because only three such societies existed on campus, some girls were excluded from joining any. She first tried to convince her sorority to take in more members; when this failed, she tried to persuade the school administration to organize a fourth sorority. "Every girl," she said to the headmistress, "ought to have the fun of belonging to a sorority if she wants to." This also failed. She also incited a small rebellion in a class reading Henrik Ibsen's plays, when she protested that all emphasis was placed on the "safe" character of Nora in A Doll's House, while the darker character of Hedda Gabler and the venereal disease talked about in Ghosts were skipped over.

As much as Amelia enjoyed her first experience of living with other women, she was nevertheless markedly different from most of them and seemed to be searching for a life that was outside of the norm. During this period she became even more career-minded and made a notebook of newspaper clippings on women around the world who were doing jobs previously reserved for men, such as a lookout for a forest service, a doctor, a lawyer in Bombay, India, a bell ringer, a Toronto woman who was a bricklayer, and several bank presidents.

Not everything in Amelia's life, however, was career-oriented. On her summer vacation in 1917, Amelia spent time with her family in Kansas City and then traveled to Camp Gray on the eastern shore of Lake Michigan to vacation with some friends. Although conditions were rather primitive, with no electricity or hot water, she had a wonderful time and showed an interest in boys for the first time. One in particular seems to have attracted her. In a letter to her mother she wrote:

There are several very nice girls of about fifteen or so and a small group of older women and one boy of twenty-three who is exceptionally fine and who has been very nice to me whenever he could. He is an old family friend of the Tredwells and he and his mother are here for a while longer. I like him so much. His father was on Roosevelt's personal Rough Rider staff and was very well known. Gordon Pollack is his name. He is very interested in photography and was offered a position as war photographer but refused to go into the aviation corps. He has made several dozen studies of me which I am anxious to see and which I hope will be good.

America was embroiled in World War I when Amelia returned to Ogontz in the fall of 1917 for her senior year, and she became very active in the war effort. Secretary of a campus Red Cross chapter, she also sold Liberty Bonds, took a course in surgical dressing, and organized a movement to forgo class rings and give the money instead to the Red Cross. She still felt, however, that she wasn't doing enough. For her Christmas vacation she joined her mother

Amelia's graduation picture from the Ogontz School. Amelia actually left Ogontz before graduating.

and sister in Toronto, where Muriel was attending St. Margaret's College. At Ogontz she had not been directly exposed to the war, but in Toronto she could not avoid it. She later wrote in her autobiography, *20 Hrs., 40 Mins.*:

In every life there are places at which the individual, looking back, can see he was forced to choose one of several paths. These turning points may be marked by a trivial circumstance or by one of great joy or sorrow. . . . Four men on crutches, walking together in King Street in Toronto that winter, was a sight which changed the course of existence for me. The realization that war wasn't knitting sweaters and selling Liberty Bonds, nor dancing with handsome uniforms, was suddenly evident. Returning to school was impossible, if there was war work that I could do.

In fact she did return briefly to Ogontz, but by February 1918 her mother had allowed her to leave the school without graduating and return to Toronto. Amelia took an intensive first aid course and enrolled in the Voluntary Aid Detachment (V.A.D.).

She was assigned to Spadina Military Hospital, which was an old and small college building converted to war use. Her twelve-hour days consisted primarily of making beds, carrying trays, giving back rubs, and cheering up the soldiers. When the director of nurses discovered that she had a knowledge of chemistry, she was promoted to the diet kitchen. Amelia felt that patient morale might be slightly improved if meals were made less dreary. Approaching the head dietician, an imposing Englishwoman named Mrs. Waldron, she asked that stewed tomatoes be alternated with the turnips and parsnips that were invariably served.

Amelia as a volunteer nurse
in Toronto, 1917

She presented figures showing that tomatoes cost less than a cent more per serving, reminded Mrs. Waldron that they could be served to anyone not on a nonacid diet, and finished by stating, "And, Mrs. Waldron, tomatoes are so much cheerfuller." Tomatoes began to appear at meals. She also waged war against rice pudding, which was served so often that one day two soldiers in adjoining beds emptied it onto their trays into mounds and marked the mounds with bent matches that formed the letters R.I.P. (Rest in Peace). Amelia pressed for a different kind of pudding, and the whole staff joined in to help, contributing molds and much rationed cherries and orange slices. When word got out that Amelia was responsible for the change, the same two soldiers printed the message "Ray, Ray, USA" (Hurray, Hurray, USA) on a cleaned tray.

Despite such humorous occurrences, Amelia's nursing experience left her with a horror of war that deepened her already pacifist leaning. "There for the first time," she would later write, "I realized what the World War meant. Instead of uniforms and brass bands, I saw the results of four years' desperate struggle; men without arms and legs, men who were paralyzed and men who were blind."

Whenever Amelia had a Saturday afternoon off, she and Muriel, who was still studying at St. Margaret's, would go riding at a local stables. One day Amelia expressed an interest in riding a dappled gray that she had not seen before, but the groom told her that he had been mishandled by the cavalry colonel who had previously owned him, and the horse was considered dangerous. Amelia began going by the stable every day after work to pet the gray horse or give him a piece of an apple, and at the end of the month she was riding him. Captain Spaulding, of the Royal Flying Corps, had ridden with the two women several times and admired Amelia's skill with the horse. "Watching the way you ride that horse reminds me of the way I have to fly my plane," he told her. He then invited Amelia and Muriel out to the corps airfield. Amelia had hoped to be able to go up in a plane herself, but it was strictly forbidden for civilians to do so. Soon, however, she was spending many of her free hours watching pilots being trained at the airdrome. She wrote later in *20 Hrs., 40 Mins.* that it seemed to her that "one of the few worthwhile things that emerged from the misery of war . . . those months in Toronto roused my interest in flying, although I did not realize it at the time. Perhaps it was the glamour of the environment, the times, or my youth. Aviation had come close to me."

The war finally ended, but in 1918 a great flu epidemic broke out, and Amelia stayed on her feet, working in the pneumonia ward. The long hours and grueling work eventually caught up with her, and she became seriously ill with the disease. After a long convalescence, she joined her mother and Muriel in Northampton, Massachusetts. Mrs. Earhart had again separated from her husband, and Muriel was now attending Smith College.

Not feeling quite well enough to attend school full time, but too well to just sit around, Amelia enrolled in a class in automobile engine repair at Smith. The skills she acquired there aided her greatly in her flying career. She also spent $25 on a used banjo and found a musician to teach her how to play it. These activities kept her contented until she had fully regained her strength. Her nursing experiences in Toronto had inspired Amelia to try medicine, so she entered Columbia University in New York as a premed student in the fall of 1919.

As usual, she jumped fully into university life by not only taking a full course load in her field but also by auditing other "luxury" courses in such areas as French poetry. In addition, she hiked in the surrounding countryside and explored the many cultural advantages of New York City. "Students in New York," she would later write in *The Fun of It*, "can get so much with so little if they really wish. . . . the steps in the gallery of Carnegie Hall are really not uncomfortable. . . ." She also explored the campus of Columbia in much the same way that she had explored Missouri caves as a girl. "I was familiar with all the forbidden underground passageways which connected the different buildings of the University. I think I explored every nook and cranny possible. I have sat in the lap of the gilded statues which decorated the library steps, and I was probably the most frequent visitor on the top of the library dome. I mean the top." She also did well in her academic work. One of her professors, a biologist, would later comment that "she grasped the significance of an experiment, mentally assayed the results, and drew conclusions while I was still lecturing about setting up the experiment. She was a most stimulating student. . . . I feel that had Amelia not become caught up in the adventure of flying, she would have found equally challenging frontiers to conquer in the laboratory." Most friends, however, felt that her sense of adventure was too strong to permit a medical career. And finally Amelia herself came to the same conclusion:

It took me only a few months to discover that I probably should not make the ideal physician. Though I liked learning all about medicine, particularly the experimental side, visions of its practical application floored me. For instance, I thought among other possibilities of sitting at the bedside of a hypochondriac and handing out innocuous sugar pellets to a patient with an imaginary illness. . . . This picture made me feel inadequate and insecure. . . .

The desire to serve humanity was strong in Amelia, but her innate restlessness was even stronger. Although she probably was put off by the thought of treating hypochondriacs, the years of drudgery that a medical career would entail was probably a greater deterrent to her becoming a doctor.

By the summer of 1920, her father had moved his law practice from Kansas City to Los Angeles. Her mother joined him there, but almost immediately friction between the two arose. Amelia's parents begged her to come out to Los Angeles, perhaps feeling that they needed a buffer. Amelia agreed to go but told Muriel that later she would "come back here [to the East Coast] and live my life."

FLIGHT

4

In the summer of 1920, Amelia, now almost twenty-three, joined her parents in Los Angeles. She planned to continue with medical research at a school in California as well as try to prevent her parents from separating. But one day she went with her father to see the Long Beach air show. Fascinated by what she saw, and spotting a man in a flying uniform, she said to her father, "Please ask him how long it takes to learn to fly."

Her father talked to the young man and came back to her. "Apparently it differs with different people, but the average seems to be from five to ten hours."

"And did you ask him how much lessons cost?"

"No, but I will."

He spoke with the young man again.

"He says a thousand dollars. But why do you want to know?"

Amelia said she wasn't sure. But later that evening, while washing up the dinner dishes, she stated that she wanted to learn to fly. Her father stated flatly that he didn't have a thousand dollars, so Amelia convinced him to at least let her go up once. They drove out to the local airfield and found a pilot named Frank Hawks. Hawks was an Iowa-born pilot who would later set over two hundred records for speed flying on cross-country routes. Amelia paid him one dollar to take her up, in his plane. Hawks was willing, as long as another pilot went along to keep his "lady passenger" from becoming hysterical and jumping out.

"As soon as we left the ground," Amelia later wrote, "I knew I had to fly by myself. Miles away I saw the ocean. . . . The Hollywood hills smiled at me over the edge of the cockpit. . . . We were friends, the ocean, the hills, and I." No other experience had ever or would ever involve her so totally.

She immediately made plans to earn the money needed for lessons. To this end she landed a job at the local telephone company. Sorting messages and running errands during the week, she spent all weekend at the Long Beach airfield, which was located outside of Los Angeles. The trip involved a long bus ride and several miles of walking each way, but she did it gladly.

Flying in those days was still pretty much in its infancy. Ever since the Wright brothers had first flown at Kitty Hawk in 1903, flying had been a risky business. The First World War, of course, had brought flying to the forefront of the nation's consciousness, and barnstormers, or stunt pilots who traveled the country and thrilled onlookers with their skills, kept it there. Women had already begun to make tentative forays into the field. A Frenchwoman named Raymonde de Laroche obtained her pilot's license in 1910. She was the first woman in the world to do so. The first American woman to do this was journalist Harriet Quimby in 1911, who a year later became the first woman to fly the

Above: (left to right) Orville, Catherine, and Wilbur Wright. Below: the Wright Flyer rises into the air on December 17, 1903. Orville is at the controls while Wilbur watches from the ground.

English Channel. Unfortunately, Quimby was killed less than three months later in an air accident near Boston. Despite her short career, she managed through her writing to advance the cause of aviation as a serious enterprise and also to plead the cause of women in it.

Other women took up this challenge. Altitude and endurance records were set by German flier Melli Beese, who opened her own flying school in Berlin and was responsible for training dozens of German male pilots. Hilda Hewlett, the first woman to get her pilot's license in England, trained fighter pilots in World War I, and the American Marjorie Stinson instructed many Canadian pilots for the British Royal Flying Corps. Stinson's sister Katherine became a famous stunt flier and gave many exhibitions in the United States, England, China, and Japan. Perhaps the most famous female flier prior to World War I was Ruth Law, who set in 1916, among other records, the American nonstop cross-country record for both men and women and the world nonstop cross-country record for women.

Amelia's first instructor was Neta Snook, who was the first female graduate of the Curtiss School of Aviation. She was impressed enough by Amelia's almost instinctive command of the aircraft to agree to teach her immediately and be paid later. In an attempt to be "just another flier," both women dressed appropriately for the airfield, if somewhat oddly for women of the era. "In those days," one old-time pilot remarked, "we were not quite sure as to whether 'Snooky' was a man or a woman, as few of us saw her except in a pair of dirty coveralls, her reddish hair closely cropped, and her freckled face usually made up with the assistance of airport dust and a dash of grease. . . ." Amelia wore jodhpurs and riding boots and cut her long hair. She spent $20 on a leather coat, then, deciding that it looked too new, started sleeping in it to give it wrinkles and a worn appearance. Amusing as this behavior seemed to her family, the need behind it was real—to be accepted as just another pilot.

Neta taught Amelia how to read instruments and perform the basic airplane maneuvers, such as how to fly on course and how to land, and what to do if her plane stalled or went into a spin. Amelia slowly began to gain confidence and feel a sense of accomplishment she had never before experienced. Eager to take more lessons, she decided to get a better paying job and so began driving a truck for a sand and gravel company. At this point, Mrs. Earhart decided to let Amelia have some money, but when Amelia hurried to the airfield to tell Neta the good news, she learned that the pilot, desperately needing money, had sold her plane. Neta referred her to John Montijo, an ex-army flier, to continue her lessons. He was a skilled and experienced pilot and an excellent teacher. It was with Montijo that Amelia began to study aerial aerobatics. These techniques, which the public thinks of as being only for stunt pilots, actually contribute much to any pilot's flying skills. The rolls, loops, spins, and stall turns, which seem like so much daredevilry, actually help a pilot to recover from any problem that can occur in midair. In addition, Amelia continued to learn, as she had from Neta, the mechanics of the plane itself—how to take it apart, put it together, and oil and repair an engine. Her earlier Smith College course in auto mechanics came in particularly handy at this point.

Finally John decided that she was ready to solo. She expertly took the Kinner biplane up to 5,000 feet (1,500 m) but made what she called an "exceptionally poor landing." She comforted herself with what John had once told her: that no landing was poor if the pilot was able to walk away from the plane.

In the meantime, her life was not all flying. Edwin Earhart had renounced drinking, become a Christian Scientist, and through his revived law practice had become a relatively stable member of the community. Money was still scarce, however, and the family decided to take in three young men as boarders. One of them was Sam Chapman, a chemical engineer, who became Amelia's first serious romantic interest. Sam was a "quiet, well-read New Englander" from Marblehead, Massachusetts, and a graduate of Tufts University in Medford, Massachusetts. He and Amelia shared many common interests, such as books, plays, tennis, swimming, and even politics. Both were interested in the Socialist doctrine of the IWW (Industrial Workers of the World) and together attended a rally that ended in a police raid. Sam wanted a conventional wife, however, and Amelia doubted that she could ever be that. She had just acquired a small, used Kinner Canary biplane for her twenty-fifth birthday, July 24, 1922. Shortly thereafter, by flying to 14,000 feet (4,200 m), she set a new altitude record for women. This seemed much more important to her than any romantic ideas.

In the meantime, Edwin invested the last of Amy Earhart's inheritance in a mining venture, with the hope of building this inheritance up to a substantial sum. As the mine was beginning to prosper, however, a flash flood filled the quarry, and without pumping equipment, all was lost. At this point, Edwin and Amy Earhart decided to divorce. Muriel decided to return East to work and try to complete her bachelor's degree at the Harvard University Summer School. Amelia tried to convince everyone that she should fly herself and her mother East, but that plan was firmly vetoed by everyone, so she sadly decided to sell the Kinner Canary. In its place she bought a bright yellow Kissel touring car, which had a convertible top and a running board on each side. In the late spring of 1924 she and her mother toured the West, visiting such places as Yosemite and Yellowstone National parks. They then stopped and visited with relatives in the Midwest and finally joined Muriel in Medford, a quiet, former shipbuilding town 5 miles (8 km) north of Boston.

Amelia's restlessness continued, however. Thinking that

medical research might be preferable to a medical practice, she went back to Columbia for a semester but decided this was a dead end. For a short time she taught English to foreign students in Boston, then discontinued this to attend summer school at Harvard. Finally she decided that social work might be the answer, so she interviewed with Marion Perkins, head worker at Denison House, the second oldest settlement house in Boston. It was located on Tyler Street, which was populated by Italian, Syrian, Chinese, and Irish immigrants. Perkins later wrote about her first contact with Amelia:

A tall, slender, boyish-looking young woman walked into my office in the early fall of 1926. She wanted a job and a part-time one would do, for she was giving a course in English under the university extension. Most of her classes were in factories in Lynn and other industrial towns near Boston. She had no real experience in social work but she wanted to try it, and before I knew it I had engaged her for half-time work at Denison House. She had poise and charm. I liked her quiet sense of humor, the frank direct look in her grey eyes.

It was some time before any of us at Denison House knew that Amelia Earhart had flown. After driving with her in the "Yellow Peril," her own Kissel roadster, I knew that she was an expert driver, handling her car with ease, yes more than that, with an artistic touch. She has always seemed to me an unusual mixture of the artist and the practical person.

Amelia had never studied anything involving social work in college, but she had strong convictions about its nature, which were perhaps intensified by contact with the IWW. "Social work does not begin and end with philanthropy," she later wrote. "Social work to me is essentially education, for it is synonymous with the ability to make adjustments to poverty, illness, illiteracy or any other morbid condition;

Amelia with children from Denison House

and in order to make such an adjustment competently, the first requisite is a sound education. Social service should be preventative rather than curative."

Amelia went from working part-time at the settlement house to becoming a full-time resident there. She directed both school-age girls and the pre-kindergarten. She also assisted in any number of other projects, often in rather unusual ways. Helping with a carnival that was a benefit for Denison House, she not only agreed to fly over Boston and drop publicity pamphlets but also drove the "Yellow Peril" on nearby streets to deliver handbills while simultaneously grinding a battered hand-organ.

Sam Chapman came to Boston and obtained a job with the Boston Edison Company, and he and Amelia began to consider getting married. The two went on many outings with Muriel and her friend Albert Morrissey to Marblehead, where Sam had just inherited a beautiful old house. When Amelia was appointed a resident worker and moved into an apartment in Denison House, Sam was sure that she would have little or no time for him. He mistakenly thought that she was dissatisfied with his hours at Boston Edison and offered to get another job if she would leave her job and marry him. The offer only annoyed Amelia. She told Muriel, "I don't want to tell Sam what he should do. He ought to know what makes him happiest and then do it, no matter what other people say." She soon decided to end their semiofficial engagement. She had little time to dwell on the situation, as more and more of her life was absorbed by settlement work. She particularly regretted that the hard life suffered by the "furiners" (foreigners) in her area meant that the children never had a carefree childhood, and she spent hours driving them in her Kissel to various outings and picnics.

In spite of her hectic schedule, however, flying was still important to Amelia. She joined the Boston chapter of the National Aeronautic Association, eventually becoming its vice president. She also knew the local fliers and began to

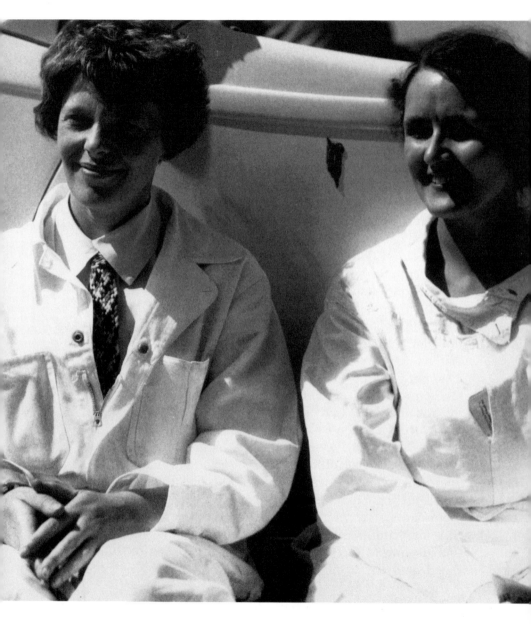

Ruth Nichols (right) with Amelia Earhart in 1933

work with flier Ruth Nichols on plans for a flying organization for women. She and Nichols formed a friendship that lasted until the end of Amelia's life and was never marred by their inevitable competitions. Nichols later noted, "Again and again, Amelia and I planned the same flights at the same time, each without knowledge of the other's intentions."

Amelia became more and more involved in social service, and there was no indication that her busy life was about to change direction. She was even planning to write a book with another social worker on the teaching of English to foreigners. But one day she received a phone call that was to forever interrupt that project.

5

In the spring of 1928, George Palmer Putnam, of the publishing house that bore his name, was visited by Hilton H. Railey, a former captain in the U.S. Army. Railey, the grandnephew of Mrs. Jefferson Davis (wife of the president of the Confederacy during the Civil War), was born in New Orleans. He became a newspaperman and worked in New Orleans, Philadelphia, and New York. He first met Putnam while serving in the Army during World War I. In 1920 Putnam and the government sent Railey to Poland on a double mission—to report on the newly independent country for the *New York Evening Mail* and to check out its military situation for the Polish minister to the United States. Putnam wanted to publish a book about modern Poland, and the two men became friends as a result of the project.

By 1928 Railey was head of a public relations firm with offices in Boston, Philadelphia, and New York. Among his clients were such pioneers of aviation as Richard E. Byrd, who would conduct explorations of the North and South poles, and Ruth Nichols, the most famous female flier until Amelia. These fliers needed publicity in order to get funds to back their ventures.

Putnam had heard a rumor that the former Amy Phipps

of Pittsburgh, who had married an Englishman named Frederick Guest, had recently bought Commander Byrd's Fokker aircraft and planned to fly the Atlantic. Putnam wanted Railey to try to verify this rumor. Railey later wrote in his memoir *Touch'd with Madness* that when he asked Putnam why he wanted to know, Putnam replied:

Hell, if it's true we'll crash the gate. It'd be amusing to manage a stunt like that, wouldn't it? Find out all you can. Locate the ship. Pump the pilots. Chances are they know all about it. Maybe there's nothing to it . . . Suit yourself. But let me know what you pick up. Telephone me if it's hot.

Returning to Boston, Railey managed to find out that Byrd's aircraft was being refitted with pontoons, or portable floats, in place of the wheels, at the East Boston Airport. He also found out that two fliers from out of town, Wilmer "Bill" Stultz and Louis Gordon, were staying at Boston's Copley Plaza Hotel.

Bill Stultz, who was twenty-seven, had served with the 634th Aero Squadron during World War I. He had then joined the Navy and flew seaplanes for several years. Later he had taken forty planes to Brazil for Curtiss Airlines and had given Brazilians flying lessons, worked as a test pilot, and been a member of the Gates Flying Circus. Stultz was an excellent pilot, navigator, and radio operator, but he was hampered by a drinking problem.

Lou "Slim" Gordon, a mechanic from Texas, was twenty-six and also army-trained. In 1921 he had served as a mechanic on bombers that had sunk two obsolete battleships. General Billy Mitchell had done this in hopes of convincing the U.S. General Staff of the need of more airpower in war. Since getting out of the Army in 1926, Gordon had served as a mechanic for the Philadelphia Rapid Transit Air Service.

Stultz told Railey that they were secretly preparing for

a transatlantic flight. The secrecy was to avoid having any-one else attempt the flight before they could take off. He also let slip that his contact with the group sponsoring the flight was Mrs. Guest's attorney, a man named David T. Layman. Through Layman, Putnam and Railey were able to get all necessary details about the flight and to persuade the sponsors to allow them to manage it.

Charles Lindbergh's flight in 1927 had captured the imagination of the world. In spite of the number of fliers who had perished by undertaking the same adventure—nineteen in 1927 alone—Amy Guest wished to have a woman cross the Atlantic by air and to land in England. Deeply loving both her countries, she hoped the flight would improve Anglo-American relations. Despite the fact that she was middle-aged, she had originally planned to make the flight herself, but her children, afraid for her safety, had talked her out of it. Mrs. Guest then decided to finance the flight instead, but insisted that "an American girl of the right image" be on board.

Railey's first task was to find such a person. An ac-quaintance of Railey's, a retired rear admiral in Boston, knew "a young social worker who flies. I'm not sure how many hours she's had, but I do know she's deeply inter-ested in aviation and a fine person. Call Denison House and ask for Amelia Earhart."

When the call came one afternoon in April 1928, "the neighborhood" was just coming in for games and classes. Not wanting to be disturbed in the midst of her busy schedule, Amelia told the person who took the call that she could not be disturbed unless it was very important. When she finally went to the phone, a male voice identified itself as Hilton Railey and asked if she "was interested in doing something aeronautic which might be hazardous." Amelia had received several such offers before—usually from bootleggers who wanted her to transport their illegal alcohol—so at first she was not impressed. However, when Railey gave her references that included First Army Headquarters and Commander Byrd, she grew interested and agreed to see Railey at his office later the same day, provided she could bring Marion Perkins along. Despite her own warnings to herself not to get too excited, she could hardly wait to get to the interview, and Perkins had to warn her not to speed in the yellow Kissel car.

Railey later wrote that almost from the moment he saw her, he had the sense that here was the young woman for whom he had been searching—young, personable, possessing a pleasant voice and a competent manner. He was pleased that she had logged more than 500 hours in the air, which indicated that she was technically competent enough as a pilot to be involved in the enterprise. But best of all, she closely resembled Charles Lindbergh, and Railey was smart enough to know the effect that small detail would have on the public. Her only disadvantages were that she was not skilled at instrument flying, which the flight would require, and that she had little experience at flying tri-motored planes. Despite these facts, she expressed a wish to take her turn at the controls. She was warned that although the pilot would be paid $20,000 and the mechanic $5,000, she would receive no fee. Even the money she might earn by writing newspaper stories about the flight would have to be turned over to her sponsors. The fact that the experience would be her only reward seemed not to bother Amelia at the time. She also assured Railey that should a disaster occur, she would not hold the sponsors responsible.

Having satisfied Railey that she was the right person for the flight, Amelia then traveled to New York to be interviewed by Putnam, Layman, and Amy Guest's brother. Amelia later remarked that this interview found her in a "curious situation. If they did not like me at all, or found me wanting in too many respects, I would be deprived of the trip. If they liked me too well, they might be loath to drown me. It was, therefore, necessary for me to maintain an attitude of impenetrable mediocrity. . . ."

Because of the need for secrecy, Amelia was not told

when the plane would take off, who was financing the project, or even who the other members of the crew would be. In spite of the uncertainty that these mysteries added to an already dangerous prospect, she remained enthusiastic about the flight. The three men quizzed Amelia intensely "about my education, and work, and hobbies. I had the feeling they liked me, but, as they did not minimize the hazards of the trip, maybe that isn't good, because they may not want to put me in a situation where I may be dropped in the cold Atlantic's Davy Jones' locker. I realized that they were making me talk to see whether I dropped my 'g's' or used 'ain't,' which I'm sure would have disqualified me as effectively as failing to produce a pilot's license." This meeting was the first between Amelia and the man who would eventually become her husband, George Putnam. He didn't seem too impressed with her, she reported later to Marion Perkins, because he deposited her on the train back to Boston like a "sack of potatoes. Didn't offer to pay my fare back home either!"

Layman wrote Amelia almost immediately to let her know that she had been chosen for the flight and to give her more details about it in addition to those outlined by Captain Railey in the initial interview. Commander Byrd was to act as technical consultant, but once the *Friendship* had actually taken off, Amelia would be responsible for making flight decisions.

Since she would not be the actual pilot, exactly why the decision was made to have her "command" the flight is not clear; perhaps it was a public relations move or the result of worry over Stultz's drinking. In any case, the flight was scheduled for mid-June. Amelia wrote Railey the following letter on May 2:

It is very kind of you to keep me informed, as far as you are able, concerning developments of the contemplated flight. As you may imagine, my suspense is great indeed.

Please do not think, however, that I hold you respon-

*sible in any way for my own uncertainty. I realize that you
are now, and have been from the first, only the medium of
communication between me and the person or persons who
are financing the enterprise. For your own satisfaction may
I add here that you have done nothing more than present
the facts of the case to me. I appreciate your forbearance
in not trying to "sell" the idea and should like you to know
that I assume all responsibility for any risks involved.*

The plane was being made ready in the interim and was
taken on a number of short flights over Boston Harbor to
determine its load capability. This was necessary because
the overseas flight would require two extra gas tanks holding 900 gallons (3,400 l) of gas. The flights also allowed
the crew to test the precision of the plane's instruments.

Amelia was not part of this. She was too well known
around the Boston hangar to take the chance of being seen
testing the plane. The press had been told that the Fokker,
which had been christened the *Friendship*, was still owned
by Commander Byrd and was being readied for an expedition to the South Pole. It was some weeks before Amelia
even got to see the big monoplane, which had been built
in Germany and resembled the bomber planes used by the
World War I Luftwaffe. She later wrote: "the ship's
golden wings, with their spread of seventy-two feet, were
strong and exquisitely fashioned. The red orange of the
fuselage, though blending with the gold, was not chosen for
artistry but for practical use. If we had come down orange
could have been seen further than any other color." She
also met her compatriots for the flight—Bill Stultz and
Slim Gordon.

The flight plan called for the three to fly the *Friendship*
to Trepassey Bay, Newfoundland, from which point they
would attempt to reach England. The weather, however,
delayed their initial flight. For more than two weeks a
weather pattern prevailed that left Boston stormy but the
mid-Atlantic clear, or vice versa. Everyone waited anx-

The Fokker aircraft called the Friendship, *the plane that carried the first American woman across the Atlantic Ocean by air. Seen in the open doorway is Amelia, checking the weather before takeoff from Trepassey Bay, Newfoundland.*

iously, but the frustration seemed to hit Bill Stultz worst of all, and he began drinking. Slim Gordon, accustomed to Stultz's behavior, assured everyone that all would be well once they took off. Amelia, reminded of her father's problem with alcohol, was particularly uneasy, but she did not complain. Putnam and Railey did their best to distract her by taking her out to dinner and to the theater, and for long drives in the country. Twice during this period the three fliers met at 3:30 A.M. in the lobby of the Copley Plaza, where Stultz and Gordon were staying, and drove to the East Boston Airport with their gear, hoping to be able to leave. Both times thick fog and a lack of wind made it impossible for them to take off for Newfoundland.

During this period of waiting Amelia wrote what she called her "popping off" letters, short notes to her parents to be given to them by Putnam only if the plane failed to land on the other side of the Atlantic. Each note contained examples of purposeful misspelling, an impish habit she used in informal letters to family and friends. To her mother she wrote "Even tho [*sic*] I have lost the adventure it was worth while. Our family tends to be too secure. My life has really been very happy and I didn't mind contemplating its end in the midst of it." Her letter to her father was more cheerful:

May 20, 1928

Dearest Dad:

Hooray for the last grand adventure! I wish I had won but it was worth while anyway. You know that.

I have no faith we'll meet anywhere again, but I wish we might.

Anyway, good-by and good luck to you.

Affectionately, your doter [sic],

Mill

On June 4, 1928, the *Friendship* finally lifted off from East Boston Harbor. Amelia kept the logbook and recorded the following notes:

Ninety-six miles out (1 hour). 2500 feet. Bill shows me on the map that we are near Cash's Ledge. We cannot see anything (if there is anything to see) as the haze makes the visibility poor. The sun is blinding in the cockpit and will be, for a couple of hours. Bill is crouching by the hatchway, taking sights.

As they approached the coast of Halifax, Nova Scotia, two hours later, Amelia did not yet know it, but she was already becoming famous. Right after the *Friendship* took off, Putnam and Railey released the news to the press that the plane was on the first leg of a flight to England with the first woman to fly the Atlantic aboard. From that moment on, Amelia was no longer a private citizen.

Halifax was only halfway to Trepassey Bay, but a dense fog forced the trio to spend the night there. As they checked into a hotel in Dartmouth and were surrounded by reporters, Amelia had her first taste of what it meant to be a celebrity. The resulting stories that appeared in the next morning's papers disturbed her with the "strange assertions they made about us all." The Boston papers carried the story that she was trying to recover her family's fortune.

The three left Halifax the next morning and reached Trepassey Bay about three that afternoon. On landing, they were greeted by an unofficial welcoming committee comprised of small boats and cheering Newfoundlanders throwing ropes at the *Friendship*. Slim Gordon, terrified that the ropes might catch in the plane's propellers, jumped on a pontoon and tried to get them to stop, while Bill Stultz cursed everyone roundly. At the same time, a gale began to come in from the sea, so everyone headed for shore.

The next day, while Gordon checked over and made repairs to the plane and Stultz worried over the delay

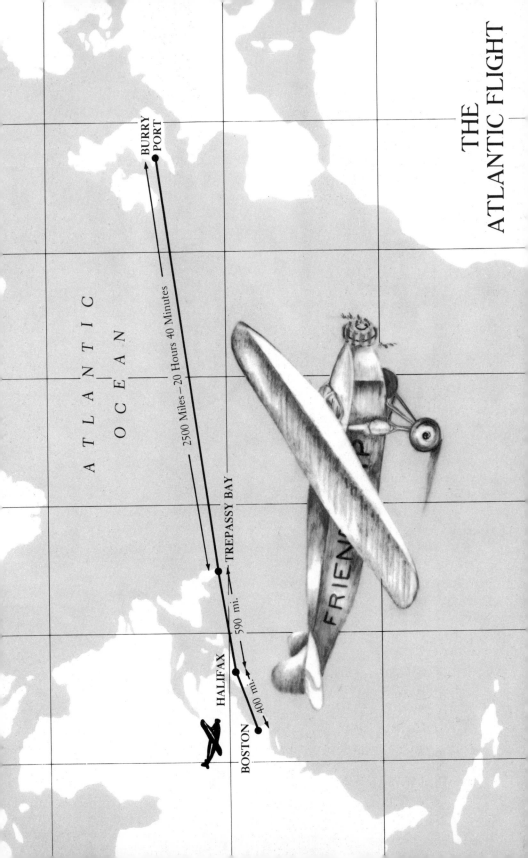

THE
ATLANTIC FLIGHT

BURRY
PORT

2500 Miles—20 Hours 40 Minutes

ATLANTIC
OCEAN

TREPASSY BAY

590 mi.

HALIFAX

400 mi.

BOSTON

FRIEND

caused by the storm, Amelia explored the village. "I could enjoy myself were it not for the anxiety about a takeoff . . . and the disgusting news of publicity." Her mother and sister now knew of Amelia's adventure, and Mrs. Earhart received a telegram from Amelia that said: KNOW YOU WILL UNDERSTAND WHY I COULD NOT TELL PLANS OF FLIGHT STOP DON'T WORRY STOP NO MATTER WHAT HAPPENS IT WILL HAVE BEEN WORTH THE TRYING STOP LOVE, A. Mrs. Earhart bravely telegraphed back: WE ARE NOT WORRYING STOP WISH I WERE WITH YOU STOP GOOD LUCK AND CHEERIO STOP LOVE MOTHER.

Actually, Mrs. Earhart had already had her first encounter with the press. Sam Chapman had been asked to break the news to Mrs. Earhart and Muriel, but before he could reach them a reporter called and asked Mrs. Earhart, "What do you think of your daughter flying overseas?" Mrs. Earhart replied, "I think she is too smart to try it," not realizing that her daughter was doing precisely that. Reporters swarmed the Medford house asking questions and demanding photographs, finally eliciting the remark from Mrs. Earhart that "in my day nice people had their names in the paper only when they were born, married, and died."

Her adventurous daughter, meanwhile, was having her own problems. Weather stalled the flight for thirteen days. Amelia and Slim, despite their frustration, managed to distract themselves by reading, playing cards, and walking the nearby beaches. Bill, however, in a fit of restlessness, began drinking heavily. The flight's backers had foreseen this possibility and had a pilot named Lou Gower waiting in Boston in case Amelia decided that Stultz shouldn't fly.

Amelia and her mother, Amy Otis Earhart.
This picture was taken a few days after
Amelia's solo flight across the Pacific
Ocean on January 12, 1935.

The decision would be hers as commander of the flight. She would later tell Putnam that she almost decided to replace Stultz. Putnam later related his conversations with her on this subject:

She considered asking us to replace Stultz. But Amelia was a scrupulously fair person, and she knew that she could not do that without great damage to Stultz; knew also that any last-minute switch might well bring the whole project tumbling down about her. How could she be sure that we— Layman and I—who knew her only slightly could trust her judgment if she did appeal to us? How could she know that we'd not simply think that here was a girl whose inexperience had caught up with her, or whose courage had failed, looking frantically for a way out?

Despite the unhappy memories of her father that Stultz's behavior must have dredged up, or perhaps because of them, Amelia tried to coax him out to go fishing or walking with her. It didn't help, and Stultz's behavior grew steadily worse. Once he even got in the plane while drunk and went careening around the harbor, endangering himself, the plane, and surrounding boats.

Finally, on June 16, the trio received the news from New York that James H. Kimball of the U.S. Weather Service, who had been keeping them informed on weather conditions, expected fair weather over the Atlantic for the next forty-eight hours. The next morning Amelia and Slim half-carried Bill down to the plane and pushed him into the cockpit. Worried about the plane's weight, they carried no luggage and reduced their fuel from 900 to 700 gallons (3,400 to 3,200 l). They carried little food with them and no change of clothing.

Nevertheless, it took four efforts to get the heavy plane out of the water and into the air. Shortly after 11:00 A.M., they were on their way.

6

Upon leaving Newfoundland the *Friendship* rose to about 1,000 feet (300 m) over the land, but soon climbed to over 5,000 feet (1,500 m) to get out of fog. At 5,000 feet it ran into a storm. Flying above the storm clouds at an altitude of 11,000 feet (3,300 m), the fliers lost sight of the ocean and did not see it again until almost the end of the flight.

Despite his hangover, Bill was alert at the controls. Amelia had a distressing moment when she saw that he had secreted a bottle in the back of the plane. Putnam later wrote in his book *Soaring Wings:*

Her instinct was to cast it through the trap door in the bottom of the fuselage. But if she did that, what might be the effect on the pilot, suddenly confronted with its absence, if he should come aft to get it? Here was a man on whose skill and self-control the lives of the three sheerly depended. She knew perfectly well that nothing must happen which would risk his concentration on the job at hand —nothing to relax the tense muscles of the jaw whose line she watched through the night and in the light of dawn as they were approaching—which? Success or disaster? There might come a moment when, to keep going, he must have the contents of that bottle. . . . As it turned out, he never wanted that bottle, and in the end, Amelia dropped it silently into the Irish Sea. . . . I think perhaps when she persistently turned the credit for the flight to Bill (where it belonged), she was moved by the knowledge that he had accomplished a perfect job in the face of personal as well as aeronautical odds.

Meanwhile, she kept herself busy with the logbook:

140 m.p.h. now. Wonderful time. Temp. 52. The heater from cockpit warms the cabin too. Bill says radio is cuckoo. He is calling now.

The rations for the flight consisted of 5 gallons (19 l) of mineral water, three large egg sandwiches, eight or nine oranges, some oatmeal cookies, a few tins of pemmican, some malted milk tablets, and some chocolate. Three oranges and some malted milk tablets were all the excited Amelia could eat during the entire flight.

Logbook:

4:15 Bill has just opened the motor to climb over this fog. We are 3800 and climbing.

Creatures of fog rear their heads above the surroundings. And what a wallop we get as we go through them.

Bill has just picked up XHY British Ship Rexmore, which gives us bearing. . . . The fog is growing patchy and great holes of ocean can be seen. XHY will inform NY of our position.

As I look out of the window I see a true rainbow. . . .

I do believe we are getting out of fog. Marvellous shapes in white stand out, some trailing shimmering veils. The clouds look like icebergs in the distance. It seemed almost impossible to believe that one couldn't bounce forever on the packed fog we are leaving. The highest peaks of the fog mountains . . . are tinted pink, with the setting sun. The hollows are grey shadowy. Pemmican is being passed or just has been. What stuff!

The pink vastness reminds me of the Mojave Desert. . . .

One of the greatest sights is the sun splashing to oblivion behind the fog, but showing pink glows through apertures in the fog. I wish the sun would linger longer. We shall soon be grey-sheathed.

We are sinking in the fog.

4000 ft.

The light of the exhausts is beginning to show as pink as the last glow of the sky. Endless foggies. The view is too vast and lovely for words. I think I am happy—sad admission of scant intellectual equipment.

I am getting housemaid's knee kneeling here at the table gulping beauty.

Amelia lay on the floor in order to write. There was nothing to sit on, as all sitting equipment had been removed to save on weight. As it began to get dark, Amelia wrote on without light, as she was afraid that the electric light in the cabin would blind the pilot. She used the thumb of her left hand to mark the starting point of a line. But as she later wrote: "The problem of this kind of blind stenography is knowing where to start the next line. It didn't always work. Too often lines piled up one on the other and legibility suffered."

Logbook:

The sea was only a respite. Fog has followed up since. We are above it now. A night of stars. North the horizon is clear cut. To the south it is a smudge.

The exhausts send out glowing meteors.

How marvellous is a machine and the mind that made it. I am thoroughly occidental in this worship.

Bill sits up alone. Every muscle and nerve alert. Many hours to go. Marvellous also. I've driven all day and all night and know what staying alert means.

We have to climb to get over fog and roughness.

Bill gives her all she has. 5000 ft. Golly how we climb. A mountain of fog. The north star on our wing tip.

My watch says 3:15. I can see dawn to the left and still a sea of fog. We are 6000 ft. high and more. Can't read dial.

Slim and I exchange places for a while. All the dragons and sea serpents and monstrosities are silhouetted against the dawn.

9000 ft. to get over them.

The two outboard motors picked up some water a while ago. Much fuss.

At least 10,000 ft. 13 hrs. 15 min. on way. . . .

We are going down. Probably Bill is going through. Fog is lower here too. Haven't hit it yet, but soon will so far as I can see from back window . . . Everything shut out.

Instruments flying. Slow descent, first. Going down fast. It takes a lot to make my ears hurt. 5000 now. Awfully wet. Water dripping in window. Port motor coughing. Sounds as if all motors were cutting. Bill opens her wide to try to clear. Sounds rotten on the right.

3000 ft. Ears not so painful. Fog awful.

Motors better, but not so good.

It is getting lighter and lighter as day dawns. We are not seeing it dawn, however. I wish I knew radio. I could help a lot.

Bill comes back to radio to find it on the blink.

We are running between the clouds still, but they are coming together. Many clouds all about. Shouldn't bother. Port motor coughing a bit. Sounds like water. We are going to go into, under or over a storm. I don't like to, with one motor acting the way it is.

How grey it is before; and behind, the mass of soggy

cloud we came through is pink with dawn. Dawn "the rosy fingered," as the Odyssey has it.

Himmel! The sea! We are 3000. Patchy clouds. We have been jazzing from 1000 to 5000 where we now are, to get out of clouds. At present there are sights of blue and sunshine, but everlasting clouds always in the offing. The radio is dead.

The sea for a while. Clouds ahead. We ought to be coming somewhat in range of our destination if we are on the course. Port motor off again. 3000 ft. 7 o'clock London.

Can't use radio at all. Coming down now in a rather clear spot. 2500 ft. Everything sliding forward.

8:50 2 Boats!!!!

Trans steamer.

Try to get bearing. Radio won't. One hr.'s gas. Mess. All craft cutting our course. Why?

The *Friendship* had come upon two small boats, which gave them hope that land was near. They then saw the steamer *America* and circled it. Since communication by radio was impossible, Bill wrote a note that asked for their position, and Amelia weighted it with an orange and dropped it. It went wide of the mark. Another note met a similar fate.

Later Amelia would discover that Captain Fried of the *America* painted the bearings of the ship on the deck every two hours whenever he knew that a crossing by air was being attempted. The secrecy of the *Friendship* flight had caught him completely unprepared, and from that time on he always kept cans of paint ready.

The decision now had to be made. With less than an hour's worth of gas left, should they try to set down by the steamer or resume their original course and hope that it could lead them to land? The crew agreed to go on and try to finish the flight.

Amelia described the next few minutes in her book *20 Hrs. 40 Mins.*:

Then we turned back to the original course, retracing the twelve mile detour made to circle the steamer. In a way we were pooling all our chances and placing everything in a final wager on our original judgment . . .

Bill, of course, was at the controls. Slim, gnawing a sandwich, sat beside him, when out of the mists there grew a blue shadow, in appearance no more solid than hundreds of other nebulous "landscapes" we had sighted before. For a while, Slim studied it, then turned and called Bill's attention to it.

It was land!

I think Slim yelled. I know the sandwich went flying out the window. Bill permitted himself a smile.

Soon several islands came into view, and then a coastline. From it we could not determine our position, the visibility was so poor. For some time we cruised along the edge of what we thought was typical English countryside.

With the gas remaining, we worked along as far as safety allowed. Bill decided to land. After circling a factory town he picked out the likeliest looking stretch and brought the Friendship *down in it. The only thing to tie to was a buoy some distance away and to it we taxied.*

The twenty-hour, forty-minute flight was over.

At first the populace of Burry Port, Wales, took no notice of the *Friendship,* even when the fliers called for help. Amelia even waved a towel out of the plane, and one man nonchalantly waved back. It took almost an hour before boats came out to see who these visitors were. The chief of police spoke first: "You be wantin' somethin'?"

"We've just come from America," Amelia answered.

"Have ye now? Well, we wish ye welcome, I'm sure."

Bill went ashore and called Hilton Railey, who was anxiously awaiting news in Southampton with the president of Imperial Airways and a representative of *The New York Times*. Meanwhile, hundreds of excited Welshmen began to gather.

When Railey arrived late in the afternoon, Amelia was "seated Indian fashion in the doorway of the fuselage and with Indian composure indifferent to the clamor ashore." He congratulated her on being the first woman to cross the Atlantic and then asked her if she were excited. She replied, "Excited? No. It was a grand experience, but all I did was lie on my tummy and take pictures of the clouds. We didn't see much of the ocean. Bill did all the flying—had to. I was just baggage, like a sack of potatoes."

"What of it? You're still the first woman to fly the Atlantic and what's more the first woman pilot."

"Oh, well," Amelia said, turning toward Burry Point and a hot bath, "maybe someday I'll try it alone."

7

The next day, which was June 18, the three fliers and Captain Railey flew to Southampton, and Amelia actually took the controls of the *Friendship* for the first time. In Southampton she met Mrs. Guest, the sponsor of the flight; Mrs. Foster Welch, the mayor of Southampton; and the president of Imperial Airways and his wife. After a civic reception for the fliers, they were taken on a tour of Southampton in a Rolls-Royce, with hundreds of cheering English people watching their every move. A cable sent by President Calvin Coolidge was given to Amelia. It praised her almost exclusively. Feeling that this was wrong, she cabled back: SUCCESS ENTIRELY DUE GREAT SKILL OF MR. STULTZ STOP HE WAS ONLY ONE MILE OFF COURSE AT VALENTIA AFTER FLYING BLIND FOR TWO THOUSAND TWO HUNDRED FORTY-SIX MILES AT AVERAGE SPEED ONE HUNDRED AND THIRTEEN MPH.

The Rolls then sped toward London, where Amelia stayed at Mrs. Guest's Park Lane mansion for two weeks. The English heartily welcomed her, and huge crowds of adoring fans followed her wherever she went. In *The Fun of It*, Amelia called her experience there "a jumble of teas, theatres, speech making, exhibition tennis, polo, and Parliament." The three fliers were given a dinner by the Air League of the British Empire. Amelia was taken by Lady

Astor to Toynbee Hall, the settlement house that had served as the model for Denison House. The American-born member of Parliament told her, "I'm not interested in you a bit because you crossed the Atlantic by air. I want to hear about your settlement work." Lady Astor also invited her to Cliveden, the Astor estate. Invited to join the party, Captain Railey wore a morning coat and silk hat, only to discover that everyone else was dressed informally. Railey proceeded to hide in the library for the rest of the day, complaining that "before the afternoon's over I'll undoubtedly be taken for the butler."

No such faux pas was committed by Amelia. Railey reported that whether

. . . laying a wreath at the Cenotaph or before the statue of Edith Cavell; whether sipping tea with the Prime Minister and Lady Astor at the House of Commons, or talking with Winston Churchill. . . . she remained herself, serious, forthright, with no bunk in her makeup. Even in those days I sensed that for all her lack of ostentation she would yet write a drama in the skies: her simplicity would capture people everywhere; in calm pursuit of an end not personal she would achieve greatness. To me, in fact, she seemed that she had been born with it.

Amelia appeared at a luncheon given by the ambassador's wife at the American embassy and another given by American correspondents. She visited the Olympic Horse Show and a military parade at Aldershot. When she went on a modest shopping spree, she was not allowed to pay for anything.

Not everyone in England was enthusiastic about the flight. The *Church Times* of London commented:

The voyage itself, for nearly all the way through fog, is a remarkable achievement made possible by the skill and courage of the pilot. But his anxiety must have been vastly

increased by the fact that he was carrying a woman passen-
ger, and as the Evening Standard *has properly pointed out,*
her presence added no more to the achievement than if the
passenger had been a sheep. Miss Earhart has been ac-
claimed by Welsh villagers, congratulated by Mr. Coolidge,
lionized in London, and she is offered large sums to appear
in the films. For us, it is all a rather pitiful commentary on
'so-called civilization'. Society cannot profit directly or in-
directly from Miss Earhart's journey. She is an international
heroine simply and solely because, owing to good luck and
an airman's efficiency, she is the first woman to travel from
America to Europe by air. A scientist has died after many
years of agony, because of his devotion to the work of heal-
ing, and for him there are only brief paragraphs in the
newspapers, while Miss Earhart has columns. Women
suffer constant discomfort and risk infection from loath-
some diseases, working for the unhappy in slums, in leper
colonies, in the fetid tropics, and their names remain un-
known. Certainly, the sense of values in the modern world
is sadly distorted.

Interestingly enough, the woman who had until a few weeks
previously been doing social work herself would probably
have agreed with most of the editorial.

She did not agree, however, with another article in the
English Review, which commented that "Not a single
aeroplane would be flying commercially today without the
Government subsidy, for the simple reason that by com-
parison with other forms of transport air transport is un-
economic. To talk vaguely of great developments which
will occur in the future is no answer, unless you can show
that the defects of air transport are technical defects which
can be overcome by mechanical means." Amelia retorted
that the newspaper's viewpoint was "reminiscent of that
when the Wrights were experimenting at Kitty Hawk." She
was certainly not blind to the fact that the immediate
benefit of the *Friendship* flight was publicity and that she

herself was to some degree being exploited by the industry, but she believed so deeply in the future of aviation that she felt it was worth whatever it took. She knew that flights such as that of the *Friendship* were the only way to pave the way for commercial air transport.

Probably the high point of Amelia's time in England was the two-hour period she spent alone in a plane over English skies. Lady Heath, an English sportswoman who had flown solo from Capetown, South Africa, to London, had offered to lend Amelia her Avian Moth so she could get away from the crowds and commitments for a time. Amelia enjoyed her time in the Avian so much that she purchased the plane from Lady Heath and made plans to ship it back to the United States.

Finally, the three heroes and their entourage sailed for home on the passenger liner the SS *President Roosevelt*. Unfortunately, this offered little relief from the tension of the previous two weeks. For one thing, the other passengers could not get over the excitement of having a real live heroine on board, and Captain Harry Manning of the *Roosevelt* finally had to set aside a deck for her use alone. The two often discussed navigation and decided that someday they should make a long flight together.

Another problem was that Bill Stultz had started drinking again. The $20,000 he had received for making the flight was no substitute for being in the air. He had brought a case of brandy on board, stayed drunk for much of the trip, and told anyone who would listen that drunkenness was "the only true form of happiness." A year later his unhappy life would end in an airplane crash at Roosevelt Field in New York.

Finally, Amelia could not forget that she had essentially been "a sack of potatoes" on the *Friendship* flight. She felt that all the honors and publicity showered upon her from the moment they had landed in Wales were out of proportion to her contribution. She confided to Hilton Railey that "someday I will have to do it alone, if only to vindi-

New York gives Amelia and the two pilots of the
Friendship *a ticker tape parade. Inset: Amelia rides
with Stultz (left) and Gordon on their way to City Hall.*

cate myself. I'm a false heroine now, and that makes me feel very guilty. Someday I will redeem my self-respect. I can't live without it."

If she didn't have her own respect completely, she certainly had that of her country. New York gave the three fliers keys to the city and a ticker-tape parade similar to the one given to Charles Lindbergh the year before. The next day Mrs. Earhart and Muriel were waiting when Amelia arrived in Boston. Kissing her mother, she said, "How are you, Ma? Hello, Sis," as though she had been away for a weekend. Asked to remove her hat, she tossed it to Muriel and said, "Here's where I get sixty more freckles on my poor nose, I guess." Boston held a parade for her, and Amelia was careful to wave to the children from Denison House who lined the route. When she was called a "gallant lady" by Commander Byrd at a dinner given in the fliers' honor, she in turn presented Stultz and Gordon as "the men who made aviation history." She had one day with her mother and sister in Medford, where she was given a small reception, and spent a few quiet hours at Marblehead with Sam Chapman. Twenty-four hours later, she was with Stultz and Gordon in Chicago, where she received her third key to a city in four days. But Stultz disappeared before the parade, so Putnam donned his leather jacket and goggles and took Stultz's place. She finally left Bill and Slim and returned to New York, probably never dreaming that this was the last time she would ever see either of them. They were about to return to relative obscurity, and her public life was just beginning.

The man who was managing this new life of Amelia's was George Putnam. From the moment the *Roosevelt* had arrived in New York Harbor, he had been ever-present. Although Amelia was not allowed to keep any fees she might receive from newspaper articles on the flight, Putnam saw no reason why she could not earn money in other ways. He had put her under contract to his publishing house for a book on her *Friendship* experience, which he envisioned as a best-seller on a par with Lindbergh's *We* (also published by Putnam), and made plans for her to write it undisturbed at his home in Rye, New York. Thirty-two cities had issued invitations to receptions, and Putnam was already planning a lecture tour for her. He began arranging articles for her to write for magazines and advised her on what commercial products to endorse. He also arranged for her to have help in answering the more than two hundred letters a day that were arriving for her. He saw all of this as publicity for the book, the publishing house, and himself. Unused to the pressures that accompanied fame, Amelia gratefully accepted the offer of the Rye house, which she grew to love both for its beauty and its privacy. She dutifully wrote her book, which she called *20 Hrs. 40 Mins.*, and dedicated it to Dorothy Binney Putnam, Putnam's wife and her hostess, of whom she grew very fond.

After she had turned in her manuscript, she felt the need to be a "vagabond in the air," so she got into her new Avian Moth and headed for Los Angeles. The trip was not without incident. Upon landing at Rogers Field in Pittsburgh, a wheel hit a shallow ditch and the plane turned over. Amelia, hanging upside down by her safety belt, calmly cut the motor, unfastened herself, and climbed out. The plane needed repairs, but a day and a half later she was on her way again.

Later on the same trip, she was flying toward El Paso, Texas, when her map flew out the window. With nothing but common sense to guide her, she followed a highway until it ended and, seeing a small town with a wide strip down its center, landed successfully on Main Street of Hobbs, New Mexico. Several local citizens helped her fold the wings of the plane and tow it to a side street for the night. The next day, still trying to get to El Paso, Amelia had two flat tires. Finally taking off, she experienced engine trouble at 4,000 feet (1,200 m). Making an emergency landing near a highway, she flagged a passing car and was towed to the nearest town. As soon as the engine was repaired, she headed west.

While in Los Angeles, she visited her father and attended the National Air Races. On her trip back East, her engine failed again, and she was forced to land in a plowed field in Utah. But she kept going, and with her return to New York she became the first woman to make a solo round-trip transcontinental flight.

Amelia then began the grueling lecture tour that Putnam had arranged for her at colleges and universities, town halls, and so on. For a number of months she kept moving from speaking engagement to social engagement. Twenty-seven cities covered in a month was not unusual, with little travel time allotted, much less any time to rest. She had also been made an associate editor of *Cosmopolitan* and was under contract to write eight articles a year on aviation subjects. In hotel rooms or on trains, she found time to write articles with such titles as "Try Flying Yourself," "Is It Safe for You to Fly?" "Shall You Let Your Daughter Fly?" and "Why Are Women Afraid to Fly?"

Deluged with offers to promote various commercial products, Amelia refused many, including a request to have her picture on tins of canned rabbit. One promotion that Amelia did become involved with was an endorsement for cigarettes, which stated that it was the brand carried on the *Friendship*. As a nonsmoker, Amelia had first turned down the offer, but the company refused to pay Stultz and Gordon their share unless Amelia went along with it. Remembering the kindness of Commander Byrd before the *Friendship* flight, she gave the $1,500 she was paid to Byrd, to use for his second Antarctic expedition. Later, in appreciation of this gesture, Byrd presented her with the second copy of the limited edition of his book, *Skyward*.

Within a few months Amelia had earned more than $50,000 from endorsements, lectures, and her articles on aviation subjects in general. Never had she been so financially independent. Because of the enormous demands be-

George Putnam managed Amelia's busy career, which included many promotions for popular products.

ing made upon her, however, she was dependent on George Putnam to manage many other aspects of her life. Mutual friends warned her that Putnam was an opportunist who would instantly divorce his wife if he thought he could marry Amelia. Hilton Railey, upon leaving the *Friendship* party to help Commander Byrd with the financing of the Antarctic expedition, gave Amelia a piece of paper with the word "brushfire" written on it and told her to consider it a code word. She was to use it to send for him if she needed help in keeping George Putnam at bay. Amelia smiled and took the paper but never used it.

The press, meanwhile, had seized upon her friendship with Sam Chapman, and some reports even mentioned him as her fiancé. When she was approached on the subject, she told the reporter, "I am not going to announce my engagement. I have seen Samuel Chapman since I have been here, but I have seen a great many other people also." Actually, Amelia was feeling great reluctance to be married at this point. Muriel married Albert Morrissey during this period, and when Amelia was complimented at the wedding reception on the *Friendship* flight, she remarked, "I think what Pidge has just done took more courage than my flight did." No doubt her parents' example only added to her hesitation.

One good example of marriage that she was exposed to at this time was that of the Lindberghs, with whom she had become friends. She was particularly impressed with Anne Lindbergh's ability to maintain her sense of identity in spite of her husband's fame. Amelia apologized profusely to Anne for the "Lady Lindy" nickname Amelia was given, feeling that it rightfully belonged to Lindbergh's wife.

Anne Lindbergh was equally impressed by Amelia. In a letter to her sister, she commented:

She is the most amazing person—just as tremendous as C. [Charles], I think. It startles me how much alike they are in breadth. C. doesn't realize it, but he hasn't talked to her as much. She has the clarity of mind, impersonal eye, coolness of temperament, balance of a scientist. Aside from that, I like her.

As much as Amelia might have seemed like Lindbergh, in their reaction to fame the two were very unalike. Lindbergh enormously resented the publicity he received and had been known to be openly rude to the press and to the public. Amelia shrugged it off as being "part of the job." Already she was learning to conceal many of her deeper feelings behind a public mask. Although most persons were charmed by her, many sensed a remoteness behind the friendly grin. Fame never really seemed to touch her; it was simply a means to an end—flying. She never lost her sense of humor about it all, however, and told stories about herself being "recognized" as everyone from Gracie Allen to Charles Lindbergh's mother.

Through her association with Lindbergh, Amelia became involved with Transcontinental Air Transport (TAT), the forerunner of Trans World Airlines (TWA). TAT had been founded by Eugene Vidal, an ex-army pilot who would become a close friend of Amelia's. Lindbergh, who was chairman of the TAT technical committee, was convinced that more men would use airline service for business travel if their wives felt it was safe. In addition to her other speaking engagements, Amelia began traveling both to businessmen's groups and to women's groups to convince them that flying was a safe means of transportation. When not flying herself, she used TAT planes to travel to her destinations whenever possible and often took her mother with her to show everyone how safe she regarded air travel. She and Lindbergh even talked at one point about setting up their own airline, but the plan was abandoned as being impractical.

In August of 1929, Amelia participated in the first Woman's Air Derby, in which twenty female pilots were to fly from Santa Monica, California, to Cleveland, Ohio, for a grand prize of $2,500. In preparation for this event Amelia had sold her lightweight Avian Moth and bought a larger, heavier Lockheed Vega, considered more appropriate for long distances. The race took eight days, with prearranged stops. Despite everyone's desire to win, an

Charles Lindbergh and
his wife Anne in 1929

The women from the First National Women's Air Derby.
From left to right: Louise M. Thaden, Bobbie Trout,
Patty Willis, Marvel Crosson, Blanche W. Noyes,
Vera Dawn Walker, Amelia Earhart, Marjorie Crawford,
Ruth Elder, and Florence Lowe Barnes

atmosphere of camaraderie prevailed. When Amelia ran into a sandbank and damaged her propeller in Yuma, Arizona, the other fliers in the "Powder Puff Derby," as the media were calling it, voted to wait three hours while the damage was repaired. On the last leg of the journey, Ruth Nichols and Amelia were leading. During takeoff Ruth's plane crashed into a tractor parked at the end of the runway. Instead of taking off, Amelia immediately jumped out of her plane and ran over to help Ruth get out of the wreckage. As soon as she knew Ruth was unharmed, she took off, but she had lost her advantage. She finished third behind Louise Thaden and Gladys O'Donnell.

Unfortunately, one contestant, Marvel Crosson, was killed when her plane crashed and her parachute failed to open, but there were also some humorous incidents. Forced to land in Texas, flier Ruth Elder told Amelia, "Pretty soon I saw a nice big pasture close by a farmhouse. There were a lot of animals in it but that didn't bother me until after I had landed, when out of a clear sky I remembered my ship is painted a brilliant red! It was too late to take off. All those creatures were jogging toward me."

"What did you do?" Amelia asked.

"I prayed. Dear God, I prayed, let them all be cows."

Much publicity, although not all of it favorable, had accompanied the derby. At most of their scheduled stops they had been the recipients of banquets and local attention. In his column, humorist Will Rogers wrote: "Claremore, Oklahoma, has grabbed off another distinction, it being the only town that the race officials didn't make the poor girls stop at. They've had to land in every buffalo wallow that had a Chamber of Commerce and put up a hotdog stand."

Because of this publicity, Amelia and Ruth Nichols agreed that the time was ripe for organizing the women's flying association they had been talking about for several years. The first meeting was held in November of 1929. Hearing with increasing horror the names suggested for the organization—Lady Birds, Gadflies, Homing Pigeons, Air Dames, and even Lady Buzzards—Amelia suggested that since there were ninety-nine charter members, the name of the organization should be the Ninety-nines. Shortly thereafter, she was elected as its first president. The purpose of the organization was "to provide a close relationship among women pilots and to unite them in any movement that may be for their benefit or for that of aviation in general." Through a monthly newsletter, they kept female pilots abreast of current aviation news and opportunities for further experience and training. They also published the first monthly magazine for and about women in aviation and hosted a number of social and educational events to inform the public about it. Amelia was very proud of her involvement with the group and later dedicated her second book, *The Fun of It*, to its members.

Meanwhile, a family problem was occupying Amelia's thoughts. When she had visited Los Angeles in November of 1929, she found that her father, who had remarried and was living in a cabin 5 miles (8 km) north of the city, was happier than he had been in years but not very well. She wrote Muriel, "I'm afraid Dad may not enjoy his little cabin too long, Pidge. . . . He looks thinner than I've ever seen him, and Helen [the second Mrs. Earhart] says he has no appetite at all and tires very quickly now." When Amelia returned to Los Angeles the following February, Edwin looked even worse. For some months his illness was believed to be a stricture of the esophagus, but by September it was known to be cancer of the stomach and inoperable. Edwin died several weeks later, and Amelia wired Muriel: DAD'S LAST BIG CASE SETTLED OUT OF COURT PEACEFULLY AND WITHOUT PAIN. She wrote her mother that "He was an aristocrat as he went—all the weaknesses gone with a little boy's brown puzzled eyes."

Although Amelia was back on the lecture circuit within a few days of her father's funeral, the combination of his death and a severe case of recurrent sinusitus aggravated by flying contributed to feelings of loneliness and depression throughout the fall of 1930. Perhaps partially because of these feelings, she decided to include something new in her life—a husband.

8

The true character of George Putnam was, and has remained, a mystery. His grandfather had founded the firm that published such giants of American literature as Washington Irving, James Russell Lowell, James Fenimore Cooper, Nathaniel Hawthorne, William Cullen Bryant, and Francis Parkman.

When Putnam was a boy, the firm was being run by his father and two uncles. Like them, Putnam began his college education at Harvard, but he soon transferred to the University of California at Berkeley. In 1908, while in his early twenties, he cut himself off from his family, and with $300 in his pockets went to live in Bend, Oregon. Within a few years he was mayor of the town and editor of the local newspaper. In 1911 he married Dorothy Binney, a young woman from Connecticut, and the couple had two sons.

Putnam served in World War I and came back to his family's publishing firm after the death of his father and brother. Among his first successes were early writings of Alexander Woollcott and the novels of Ben Hecht. Putnam was fascinated by exploration, however, and he became best known for books in this field. He was interested not only in publishing books about exploration but in doing some exploring himself. In 1925 he organized and led an expedition to Greenland for the American Museum of Natural History, He also explored the Arctic and would later serve in the Air Force during World War II in the China–Burma–India theater.

Four of the ten books he wrote in his "spare time" were about travel. He was a tall, good-looking man, whose rimless glasses gave him the look of a scholar and belied his adventurous personality. Like many hard-driving individuals, he was perceived differently by different people. Some saw him as a kind of parasite, essentially hanging on to the coattails of anyone in the limelight in order to be reflected in their glory. Reporters complained later that to get a few words from Amelia they had to listen to hundreds from him. They dubbed him a "lens louse." As much as Putnam loved the limelight, however, he was capable of being a good friend and sometimes did favors he would forbid people to mention. In any case, even his worst enemy was convinced of his intelligence, energy, and ambition.

George Putnam divorced his wife in 1928 and asked Amelia a total of six times (by his own count) to marry him. If his reasons for marrying her were complex, her reasons for marrying him were even more so. She thought that she ought never to marry. Her parents' unhappy marriage had led her to mistrust the institution as a whole, and she saw her career as another impediment. "She wanted to owe no one anything—any more spiritually than financially," as Putnam wrote. "In her heart she knew too that, for good or ill, she must keep freedom in a measure which is not always possible in marriage. She had no selfish dream of the anatomy of freedom, but she did know it for an element without which she personally could not do, as some plants can do without water but cannot survive without air." Amelia had once told a friend that she saw marriage as a cage and that she preferred work or flying. However, in George Putnam she saw a man who was willing—even eager—to act as a helpmate. In her last book she wrote:

There I should add that the Friendship *flight brought me something even dearer than such opportunities. That man-who-was-to-find-a-girl-to-fly-the-Atlantic, who found me and then managed the flight, was George Putnam. In 1931 we married. Mostly, my flying has been solo, but the preparation for it wasn't. Without my husband's help and encouragement I could not have attempted what I have. Ours has been a contented and reasonable partnership, he with his solo jobs and I with mine. But always with work and play together, conducted under a satisfactory system of dual control.*

George Putnam had shown himself a master in handling her during the early furor after the *Friendship* flight and had given her refuge at his sixteen-room home in Rye, with which she had promptly fallen in love. Twenty-four miles (38.4 km) northeast of New York City, it was a large and comfortable home on the Long Island Sound, and a place where she felt removed from wearisome publicity. She saw it as a haven to which she could retreat. Putnam's abilities at raising money for her projects was probably another influence in her decision to marry him. Amelia later admitted that: "Thus for me, can joyful luxuries like low-wing monoplanes be had." So when Putnam proposed to her for the sixth time in a Lockheed hangar as they waited for her plane to warm, she nodded her head, patted his arm, and climbed on board.

They were married February 7, 1931, at Putnam's mother's house in Noank, Connecticut. Her mother had opposed the marriage, on the grounds that Putnam was too old (he was forty-three, Amelia was thirty-three) and divorced, but her objections did not deter Amelia. On the morning of the wedding, however, Amelia handed him a letter showing that she was still "unsold on marriage":

Dear GP,

There are some things which should be writ [sic] *before we are married. Things we have talked over before—most of them.*

You must know my reluctance to marry, my feeling that I shatter thereby chances in work which means so much to me. I feel the move just now as foolish as anything I could do. I know there may be compensations, but have no heart to look ahead.

In our life together I shall not hold you to any medieval code of faithfulness to me, nor shall I consider myself bound to you similarly. If we can be honest I think the differences which arise may best be avoided.

Please let us not interfere with each other's work or play, nor let the world see private joys or disagreements. In this connection I may have to keep some place where I can go to be myself now and then, for I cannot guarantee to endure at all times the confinements of even an attractive cage.

I must exact a cruel promise, and this is that you will let me go in a year if we find no happiness together.

I will try to do my best in every way.

A.E.

Putnam smiled, took her hand, and the ceremony began. Amelia was hatless and wore a worn brown suit.

Amelia need not have worried. The biggest changes were made in Putnam's life, not her own. He sold his share of the publishing house to a cousin and accepted an offer to become head of the editorial department for Paramount Pictures so he would have more free time to manage his wife's career and travel with her. (The film *Wings,* which was about the early fliers, had been produced by Paramount and was the first film to win an Academy Award.) The couple kept separate funds and divided all expenses fifty-fifty, with whatever was left over going into a mutual savings fund.

In his years with Amelia, Putnam had many money-making ideas. Amelia advertised Beechnut chewing gum, cigarettes, the Franklin automobile, Amelia Earhart lightweight airplane luggage, and a line of women's clothing that she herself designed. Her picture appeared on billboards, and the woman who had once felt gawky and self-conscious modeled clothes for Vogue. She did, however, draw the line on several projects, including the Amelia Earhart *Friendship* flight hats. These had been made by a children's clothing manufacturer for about 50¢ each and with her name on the hatband would sell for about $3. But the workmanship on the hats was poor, and Amelia told Putnam she wouldn't be "a party to cheating kids." Putnam protested that he had already signed a contract with the manufacturer, and Amelia replied that she would sue Putnam himself if he went through with it. Finally Putnam had to negotiate a cancellation of the contract. Although Amelia recognized the value of using her fame to help finance her career, she avoided projects that exploited or cheated her fans.

The Putnams enjoyed their home in Rye and used it to entertain many famous people. Two women who lived near Amelia in Rye and became particularly close friends with her were Cornelia Otis Skinner and Ruth Nichols. Amelia admired Cornelia immensely for her ability to combine her acting and writing careers with marriage. Ruth, whom Amelia had known before Rye, failed on a transatlantic flight in 1931 and was nearly killed. However, she broke Amelia's speed record of 181.157 mph (289.6 km), flying at 210.685 mph (336.9 km). in the same year and would be the first woman to fly around the world. Both women had originally been interested in medicine and social service careers, so they had interests outside aviation in common.

After her marriage, Amelia's life took on an even more feverish pace, as she continued her writing and lecturing. Her mother later said: "We neither of us had much time

for confidential talks because of schedules and things. It was utterly impossible, and I reached a stage where I felt the only time I had a chance to talk to her was when I was holding on to her coat tails." At this time Mrs. Earhart was living with Muriel and her family. Muriel and her husband were having marital difficulties based primarily on money. Amelia generously gave financial help to both her sister and mother, but she also gave Muriel marital advice that was often not well received. As much as the two sisters looked alike, they could not have been more different in temperament. Muriel was not happy in her situation, but she accepted it and tried to be content through her teaching, church work, and son. It was not in Amelia's temperament to settle for anything, and her inability to see Muriel's position led to some misunderstandings.

Amelia liked children and might possibly have had one herself except that it "took too long to make a baby." She was a good friend, however, to her two stepsons, who loved her in return. When the boys came up from Florida, where they were living with their mother, she would cancel engagements and spend virtually all her time with them.

The Putnam marriage was hardly a typical one, but George and Amelia seemed to weather it well. If Amelia's fame attracted George, he also seemed to have sincerely cared for the woman. Although it could not always have been easy to be "only the husband" of such a famous woman, he frequently acted the part with more grace than one might have expected. When the Putnams were introduced to silent-screen stars Douglas Fairbanks and Mary Pickford in Hollywood, Fairbanks and Putnam laughingly

Amelia and George on their estate in Rye, New York

introduced themselves as "Mister Pickford" and "Mister Earhart." In fact, when in 1933 it was reported that the marriage was breaking up, a family friend reading the article at the Putnam home looked out on the patio. George was giving Amelia a ride in a wheelbarrow and then dumping her on the ground, with Amelia squealing in delight.

9

Amelia was by no means living an uninteresting life. In addition to her lectures and writing, in 1931 she learned to fly an autogiro (the forerunner of the helicopter) in just a few hours and several days later took it to 18,415 feet (5,524 m) to set a new autogiro altitude record. During an appearance at the Michigan State Fair Grounds in Detroit, where she was demonstrating autogiro flight, she crashed but was not injured. In fact, the only casualty was her husband, who, in running toward the wrecked autogiro, tripped on a support wire and broke three ribs. Amelia later remarked that this incident again proved that it was safer to fly than to remain on the ground.

Despite such occurrences, Amelia could not get it out of her mind that she, who had been little more than a passenger on the *Friendship* flight, was a "fraudulent heroine" who still needed to prove herself in the field of aviation. She decided that she should make the same flight solo. So one winter morning in 1932 she put down her morning newspaper and casually asked her husband, "Would you *mind* if I flew the Atlantic?"

With Putnam's support for the idea, she decided to approach Bernt Balchen, a Norwegian flier who had accompanied Richard Byrd on his polar and Atlantic flights

*Amelia stands next to the Pitcairn autogiro after
setting a world's altitude record for autogiros in 1931.*

and was a skilled technican and family friend. The first
conversation took place on a warm April Sunday when she,
Putnam, and Balchen were playing croquet at the Rye
house. Suddenly Amelia put down her mallet and told
Balchen she wanted to solo the Atlantic. "Am I ready to
do it?" she asked. "Is the ship ready?" Will you help me?"
Balchen replied, "Yes. You can do it. The ship—when we
are through with her—will be O.K. And—I'll help." Amelia
turned away and began swinging at croquet balls with great
energy.

It took eight weeks to ready the plane for the trip. The
Lockheed Vega Amelia had purchased three years before
had developed many problems due to numerous forced
landings in it. Eddie Gorski, an expert Lockheed mechanic,

was hired by Balchen to put in a new engine. Auxiliary fuel tanks were also installed, and several new instruments—a drift indicator, two compasses, and a directional gyrocompass—were purchased. Balchen was considering an Antarctic flight, a fact that was known to the news media, so Amelia leased the plane to him to make it look as though he were preparing it for his own expedition. She and Balchen had an agreement that if either of them felt that she or the plane was not ready, the expedition would be postponed or even canceled. She therefore wanted to operate under conditions of great secrecy so that attendant publicity would not "force" her to make the flight under less than acceptable conditions and so that her mind could focus on the flight and not on the public reaction to it.

Unlike the triengine Fokker used in the *Friendship* flight, the single-engine Vega was a land plane that could accommodate only one passenger. For several years Amelia had practiced instrument flying; now she intensified her efforts at Teterboro Airport in New Jersey. (Interesting to note, the man in charge of determining the correct fuel mix at Teterboro was an army pilot named Major Edwin Aldrin. His son "Buzz" Aldrin would become a member of the *Apollo* crew that was the first to land on the moon.)

In mid-May, the work on the plane and Amelia's training were finished, and nothing remained but to wait for good weather. Word finally came, on the morning of May 20, 1932, that the weather was clear enough to get them to Newfoundland, the point of departure. Amelia raced home to Rye, slipped into jodhpurs, a white silk shirt, a windbreaker, and a blue-and-brown scarf. Taking only a toothbrush and comb, she stopped in the kitchen and told the housekeeper not to prepare dinner that evening. She got back to Teterboro at 2:55 that afternoon and twenty minutes later was aloft, with Balchen at the controls, Gorski in the cockpit beside him, and Amelia herself sleeping on the cabin floor behind the extra fuel tank. They flew to St. John's, Newfoundland, stayed overnight, and then flew on to Harbour Grace, Newfoundland, the next day, where they waited for further weather reports. When the go-ahead was given, Balchen gave her the flight plan and final instructions. Finally, she looked at him with a small smile and said, "Do you think I can make it?" Balchen smiled back and said, "You bet." She climbed into the cockpit and was off.

For several hours there was good weather, and Amelia flew at 12,000 feet (3,600 m) relatively easily. Then her altimeter, an instrument that records height above ground, failed and was out of commission for the remainder of the flight. She next ran into a severe lightning storm that drove her slightly off course. Thinking that she could pull out of the clouds, she climbed for half an hour and suddenly realized she was in ice, which was dangerous because it weighted down the plane, iced up her windshield, and coated her airspeed indicator to such a degree that it began to register inaccurately. Suddenly the Lockheed went into a spin and dropped so low that Amelia suddenly saw ocean waves breaking below.

As the warmth of the lower altitude melted the ice, Amelia was able to regain control of the plane. Nothing remained but that she stay on "middle ground," trying to avoid both ice and the ocean. This necessitated flying through the "soup," or clouds, and she did not look out of the cockpit again until morning. She later commented, "Probably if I had been able to see what was happening on the outside during the night I would have had heart failure then and there, but, as I could not see, I carried on." Later she suddenly saw flames coming from a broken weld in the manifold ring of the engine. As morning dawned, she turned on her reserve tanks and discovered that she had a leaky fuel gauge. She knew that if it burned through, the plane would explode. Although she had originally planned to fly to Paris as Lindbergh had done exactly five years earlier, she recognized that she now was forced to land

The record-breaking Lockheed Electra

somewhere soon. She turned her plane northwest 'toward Ireland and, finding no airport, finally set down in a Culmore pasture surrounded by cows. She had been in the air fifteen hours and eighteen minutes, the fastest transatlantic crossing thus far. Farmer Dan McCallion came over to the plane and Amelia said, "Hi! I've come from America."

"Have you now," the farmer said.

A constable protected the plane from the curious neighbors while the farmer borrowed a car and drove Amelia to a nearby telephone. She phoned George in New York, assured him that she was all right, and asked him to contact her mother and sister. He immediately boarded the SS *Olympic* to join her in France. She drove back to the farm at which she had landed, ate a meal (she had only had tomato juice on the flight), and slept all day and all night.

When Amelia arrived at the Associated Press office in Londonderry the next day, there were already many cables and messages—from her mother, her sister, the Lindberghs, and Ruth Nichols, who wrote, "You beat me to it for the second time but it was a splendid job." In her cable, Lady Astor begged her to stay with her in London and offered her the loan of a nightgown, and President Herbert Hoover and King George and Queen Mary of England offered congratulations. Her favorite cable, though, was from Phil Cooper, who owned the dry cleaning store used by the Putnams. He said: KNEW YOU WOULD DO IT STOP I NEVER LOSE A CUSTOMER. Paramount News flew her to London, where she stayed at the American embassy with the American ambassador and his family and was followed by cheering crowds wherever she went. Shortly thereafter, she received the Certificate of Honorary Membership of the British Guild of Air Pilots and Navigators, the second such award given to a non-British subject, and met and even danced with the Prince of Wales, later Edward VIII and Duke of Windsor, at a London nightclub. During their dances together, the prince talked about flying, as he was a pilot himself. "I like to fly solo myself," he told her, "but they won't let me."

Luncheons, dinners, and receptions were given for her, and she received other awards and decorations. She met the playwright George Bernard Shaw. Amid all this, Amelia quietly noted, "I realize this flight has meant nothing to aviation," and on another occasion, "If science advances and aviation progresses, and international good will is promoted because of this flight, no one will be more delighted than I—or more surprised."

She met George Putnam in Cherbourg, France, and from there went on to Paris, where she was given an official reception by the French Senate. A humorous moment came when she finished her speech to the lawmakers by saying, "It is far more difficult to make good laws than it is to fly the Atlantic." "Ah, madame," replied the president, "when you fly the ocean, what you do is a danger only to yourself, while the laws we make are a danger to so many."

At the American embassy in Paris, Amelia was awarded the Knight's Cross of the Legion of Honor, which had been presented to Lindbergh five years earlier. In Rome, Amelia and George met Mussolini and attended a gathering of fliers who had flown the Atlantic; in Brussels, they lunched with King Albert and his queen, and Amelia was presented with the Cross of the Chevalier of the Order of Leopold.

Returning to America on the ship *Ile de France*, Amelia was once again the focus of intense publicity. In a solemn ceremony at the White House, President Hoover presented her with a gold medal given by the National Geographic Society. She was the first woman ever to receive it. In thanking the president and the society, Amelia stated: "The appreciation of the deed is out of proportion to the deed itself. . . . I shall be happy if my small exploit has drawn attention to the fact that women, too, are flying." Later she was presented with the Distinguished Flying Cross and awarded a congressional citation.

Although Amelia was received warmly by both President and Mrs. Hoover, her greatest presidential friendship was with Franklin and Eleanor Roosevelt. On a visit to the White House in April 1933, Amelia took Eleanor Roosevelt on an after-dinner flight in which both women were in their evening gowns; Amelia didn't even take off her long white kid gloves. Mrs. Roosevelt was delighted with the flight and reciprocated, at the end of the evening, by giving Amelia a spin in her new car. Amelia offered to teach Mrs. Roosevelt to fly, and Mrs. Roosevelt even went so far as to have the required medical exam and to get her student pilot permit. The president objected, however, and Mrs. Roosevelt reluctantly gave up the idea.

Not willing to rest on her laurels, Amelia turned her mind toward other air projects. Having flown her husband out to Los Angeles, where he had business, she then set

the women's transcontinental speed record, flying nonstop from Los Angeles to Newark, New Jersey, in nineteen hours, five minutes. One year later, she would break her own record. She later flew back to Los Angeles as one of three female participants in the Bendix Transcontinental air derby and finished third of all competitors. On her way home, she shaved two hours off her own record from the year before.

In the fall of 1934, Amelia and George Putnam moved to Los Angeles. Amelia was beginning to work on plans for a flight from Honolulu to California and wanted to be near the Lockheed factory where her new plane was being overhauled. Amelia had sold her Lockheed Vega to the Franklin Institute in Philadelphia and had bought a new and improved Lockheed. George Putnam's position with Paramount also necessitated that he spend more time on the West coast.

Amelia secured the services of Paul Mantz as technical adviser for the flight. Mantz was a former army pilot who had entered aviation at the end of World War I and had been hired by Paramount to do the flying stunts and air battles in *Wings* in 1928. He was a neighbor of the Putnams in Rye. A skilled technician and a brave pilot, he was a tremendous help to Amelia in her preparations for the flight.

In late December of 1934 Amelia, George, and Mantz sailed from Los Angeles to Honolulu on the SS *Lurline*, with Amelia's plane on the deck, and began final preparations for the flight. A group of Hawaiian businessmen, in an attempt to publicize the islands, had offered a $10,000 prize for the first person to make such a flight. A rival group of

Amelia and Paul Mantz, technical adviser to Amelia on this and what was to later be Amelia's last flight

businessmen, however, charged that the real purpose of the contest was to promote tariff concessions for Hawaiian sugar. This charge caused a controversy, and in a last-minute emergency meeting the businessmen asked Amelia to give up the flight. She stated that all of them knew that the rumors were untrue; to back out would be cowardice. "I intend to fly to California within this next week, with or without your support," she said, and walked out of the room. The sponsors decided to continue their support.

Four days later, on January 11, 1935, unusually bad weather around Honolulu made takeoff of the heavy Vega an uncertain prospect. Amelia learned, however, that a cycle of worse weather was moving in that could delay her for ten days or more. If she could just get past Honolulu, she would probably be fine, because the weather along her route was expected to be good.

She decided to make a try. As she taxied to the head of the runway in a field of mud, she noticed three fire engines, an ambulance, and a detachment of soldiers waiting with fire extinguishers. Undaunted, she managed to take the plane up to 5,000 feet (1,500 m), where clear skies and a smooth remaining flight awaited. There were no further problems, and she arrived in Oakland eighteen hours and fifteen minutes later—her longest flight yet.

Ten thousand people were waiting for her when she stepped out of the cockpit. With this flight she became the first person to fly from Hawaii to California, the first person to solo anywhere in the Pacific, and the first person to solo over both the Atlantic and the Pacific oceans. This 2,400-mile (3,840-km) distance is the longest overwater stretch in the world. By crossing it, Amelia proved that one could fly anywhere in the world. This flight, along with Charles Lindbergh's flight to the Orient in 1931, made possible the development of Pacific air transportation. Not content with this success, in April of the same year, Amelia became the first person to solo from Los Angeles to Mexico City, and then flew solo 700 miles (1,120 km) across the Gulf of Mexico and up the East Coast to Newark, New Jersey.

During their time in California, Amelia and George Putnam came to know many of Hollywood's legendary figures. Mary Pickford and Amelia had become such good friends that they even considered making a movie together. Amelia also became good friends with Will Rogers and Wiley Post. She and her husband were guests at Will Rogers' ranch only a few days before he and Wiley Post crashed and were killed on their Arctic Circle flight in 1935. Amelia had closely followed the details of Post's two earlier Arctic flights, because she was beginning to plan, with Paul Mantz's help, a round-the-world flight herself. Hers, however, would be at the equator, a distance of more than 27,000 miles (43,200 km). It would be the most hazardous, ambitious, and costly flight in history. Amelia and Mantz considered both a charter service and an aviation school as well, but neither of these projects came to anything.

All these plans had to be put aside, however, while Amelia fulfilled her promised lecture tour for the remainder of 1935. Her fall lecture schedule was twice as heavy as the spring had been. Amelia had also accepted an appointment as counselor and adviser in aeronautics at Purdue University, in Lafayette, Indiana. She was expected to spend a month in residence each year. This year the plan was to go in November, and she was supposed to act as a career consultant with women students. This was not the first time that Amelia had been concerned with women and careers. Once, in an attempt to determine whether menstruation had any effect on the flying capabilities of women, she interviewed women in a number of strenuous professions, such as dancing, athletic endeavors, and circus performing, and came to the conclusion that it was wrong to disqualify women on the belief that "on specific occasions their physical and nervous reaction would go to pieces." No board of medical officers, however, would accept her interviews as a valid study.

The atmosphere at Purdue, however, was far more conducive to her ideals. The president of the university, Dr. Edward C. Elliott, was a farseeing individual who was genuinely interested in career opportunities for the 800 women who were a part of the university's 6,000 students. After hearing Amelia speak on "Women and the Changing World" as part of a panel discussion in New York, he decided that Amelia could provide a good model for these women. Purdue was also the only university in the country that had its own airport as a part of its department of aeronautics.

Amelia made a very positive impression on both students and faculty. She was described as "tall, skinny, handsome, tousle-headed, smiling." Students were "transported with delight and even the most skeptical of older residents charmed." She lived in one of the women's dormitories and, except for once turning up for dinner in her overalls, obeyed the same rules as the coeds. She kept her door open for any girl who needed to talk and had a different group of women at her table for each meal.

In one of her informal lectures, she commented:

Times are changing and women need the critical stimulus of competition outside the home. A girl must nowadays believe completely in herself as an individual. She must realize at the outset that a woman must do the same job better than a man to get as much credit for it. She must be aware of the various discriminations, both legal and traditional, against women in the business world.

I cannot tell you that you will be able to bounce right out of college into your life work. I believe, under existing conditions, that it is almost impossible to do. But I believe also that doesn't greatly matter, for the business world will draw out one's aptitudes.

And so I'm inclined to say that, if you want a certain job, try it. Then if you find something on the morrow that looks better, make a change. And if you should find that you are the first woman to fuel an urge in that direction— what does it matter? Fuel it and act on it just the same. It may turn out to be fun. And to me fun is the indispensable part of work.

The students and most others on the campus were wildly enthusiastic. One professor did protest, "I'm afraid that if she keeps on, the coeds won't be willing to get married and lead the quiet life for which Nature intended them." But Dr. Elliott and the Purdue Research Foundation were so pleased with her work that they set up an Amelia Earhart fund for the purchase of a plane for her own use. She chose a twin-engined, ten-passenger Lockheed Electra transport plane. She needed a bigger, safer plane, for she had her greatest challenge still ahead of her.

LAST FLIGHT

10

The late Wiley Post had flown around the world both in 1931 and 1933. He had been making his third flight when he and Will Rogers were killed in 1935. All of his flights were made far north of the equator, but Amelia was planning to circle the globe roughly *at* the equator. The more than 27,000 miles (43,200 km) she would travel would constitute the longest flight in history, taking over a month to complete.

Originally she planned to fly east to west, from Oakland, California, to Honolulu, Hawaii, and then to Howland Island in the Pacific. From there she would go to Australia, Arabia, Africa, across the South Atlantic to Brazil, and home. The greatest difficulty of the flight would be the trek across the Pacific—trying to find Howland Island. A skilled navigator and excellent navigational equipment would be needed. Amelia's previous flying had been done without either, but "then I was aiming at continents, not small spots of land in the mightiest ocean."

Paul Mantz, who was acting as her technical adviser, was concerned about equipment. He insisted that she have a remote control system installed in the aircraft and that she gain a better knowledge of instrument flying, in which she was still weak. He installed a Link blind-flying trainer in the hangar in Burbank. This device simulated actual flight conditions in a closed cockpit, and Amelia spent weeks working with it. Mantz was also concerned about how to increase the Electra's fuel capacity. He consulted Clarence Belinn, an engineering superintendent for National Airways in Boston, who developed a cross-feed system between twelve auxiliary tanks and the main tank. This gave the Electra a capacity of 1,200 gallons (4,500 l) of fuel and a range of 2,500 to 3,000 miles (4,000 to 4,800 km).

Mantz was still worried about the problem of a navigator. Bradford Washburn, a young Harvard University professor who had led the National Geographic Society/ Pan American Airways photo flights over Mount McKinley in Alaska, agreed to come to Rye to talk to Amelia. When he found out that there would be no radio signals issued from Howland because neither Amelia nor George felt it was necessary, he refused to participate, saying that the mission was too dangerous. Amelia saw it as one more chance she had to take.

Finally, Harry Manning, who had been the captain of the SS Roosevelt when Amelia came home from England on her first transatlantic flight, volunteered to make the flight with her. Mantz was also worried about Amelia's— or anyone's—ability to stand up to the conditions on such a long trip. Despite several operations on her sinuses, they still bothered her, and this intensified fatigue on long flights. The fact that Amelia had been on a particularly difficult schedule in 1936—she delivered 136 lectures in addition to all her other activities—made him wonder if her physical resources were being pushed past her limit.

Putnam, meanwhile, had other problems concerning the flight to worry about. He arranged to have gasoline and spare parts waiting for Amelia at every point along the route of her flight, and he obtained from the embassies of the countries along the route permission for her to fly over or land without being charged with aerial trespassing. He was also, as always, in charge of raising the money needed

for the trip. He persuaded several commercial airlines to contribute to the flight on the basis that such an expedition was good advertising for them. He also arranged with Gimbels department store in New York to sell 10,000 letter covers. These red, white, and blue envelopes, which had a photograph of Amelia on them, would be carried with her and mailed back at different points in her route to collectors. The $25,000 Putnam raised was added to Amelia's speaker's fees and book royalties.

Amelia's friends could not get over the feeling that she was making a mistake. Her friend and fellow flier Jacqueline Cochran was particularly concerned about Captain Manning. Could a man who was used to navigating at sea be trusted in the air? Amelia took her advice to test Manning. She flew him out to sea from Los Angeles, flew in circles for a time, and had him give the course back to the city. The plane came back to the shoreline at least 200 miles (320 km) off course. Additional help was obviously needed.

It was found in Frederick Noonan, an ex-pilot and navigator for Pan American Airways. From the time he had left home to go to sea at the age of fifteen, Fred had been involved in navigation. During World War I he had served on a munitions carrier traveling between New York and England, and later, after joining the British Navy, was torpedoed on three separate ships. He had gone around Cape Horn seven times, three times on a windjammer and four times on steamships. He even held a first-class riverboat pilot's license on the Mississippi River.

Amelia poses in front of the meter on the right wing of the Lockheed Electra. The meter was used to supply the power to run the plane's radio transmitter.

In the years he had been involved in aviation, Noonan had developed a reputation as a skilled technician, pilot, and navigator, but he had also developed a drinking problem. He had never been known to be drunk on a flight, but Pan American had considered him a bad risk and fired him anyway. Noonan gave up drinking, met a woman he wished to marry, and wanted a chance to prove himself. Amelia, perhaps inspired by the memory of her father, decided to give him this chance.

Amelia's friends were still not convinced. Flier Louise Thaden even flew out to California to try to dissuade Amelia from making the trip, but Amelia told her: "I've wanted to do this flight for a long time . . . If I should bop off, it will be doing the thing I've always wanted most to do . . . the man with the little black book has a date marked down for all of us—when our work here is finished . . ." This fatalistic attitude in Amelia combined with a fear of getting old made her willing to take risks. Having seen an old man asking for money and saying, "It's hard to get old . . . so hard . . . ," she said to Putnam, "It's hard to be old—I think probably, G.P., that I'll not live—to get old."

On February 11, 1937, George Putnam arranged a press conference at the Hotel Barclay in New York, and Amelia told of her plans for a world flight with Captain Manning at her side. Tracing her route on a nearby globe, she laughed and said, "I feel you men have pushed me into this. You're the ones who have kept saying and saying that I was going to fly around the world until finally you've compelled me to think seriously about doing it."

Reporter Carl Allen of the *New York Herald Tribune*, a friend of Amelia's for years, spoke up and said, "Oh, come now! Nobody has pushed you into it. You know you've been wanting to do it all the time!"

"Yes, I suppose you're right," Amelia replied. "I didn't get away with that, did I?"

"What are you going for?" another reporter asked.

"Well, I've seen the North Atlantic. I've seen the

*Frederick Noonan, co-pilot and navigator of the Electra,
discusses with Amelia the flight plan that was to take them
around the world at the equator.*

Pacific too, of course, at least a part of it. But well, just say I want to fly around the globe. And I think a round-the-world flight just now should be at the Equator. . . . Such a flight has never been attempted. I'm simply going to fly as and when I can, race nothing and nobody. Eventually airplanes will find it easy to go round the world. Not only around the Equator, but around every way. Every flight, therefore, is potentially important. It may yield valuable knowledge. We can look at all flights across the Atlantic and see that each in its way has done some definite good."

Amelia took a few weeks at Jacqueline Cochran's ranch in Indio, California, swimming, horseback riding, and resting, to get into shape for the flight. Jacqueline was an excellent flier who at the time of her death in 1980 had won more aviation awards and prizes than any other flier —male or female. She was married to the financier Floyd Odlum, who contributed heavily to the world flight. Amelia was so grateful for his help that she dedicated her book on the flight "To Floyd—with gratitude for his all-weather friendship." Jacqueline believed in extrasensory perception and had even had some luck herself "locating" passenger planes that had disappeared. According to her book, *The Stars at Noon*, the two women decided that should Amelia ever be lost on a flight, Jacqueline would use her powers to try to find her.

Finally everything was in readiness. On March 17, 1937, the Electra took off from Oakland airport, headed over San Francisco's Golden Gate Bridge, and started across the Pacific toward Honolulu. Inside the plane were Amelia; Paul Mantz, who was joining his fiancée in Hawaii and would remain there; Noonan, who would assist Amelia and Manning until they reached Howland; and Manning himself, who would be dropped off in Brisbane, Australia. Amelia hoped to make the rest of the flight solo. The flight to Honolulu was uneventful, and they touched down at Wheeler Field, 2,410 miles (3,856 km) away, fifteen hours and forty-seven minutes later.

Amelia went to the house of a friend to sleep, and Mantz moved the Electra to Luke Field, which had a longer runway than Wheeler. For the Howland leg of the trip, the plane would need to carry 900 gallons (3,400 l) of fuel. The extra weight this would add to the plane meant a longer takeoff and thus required a longer runway.

The next morning, with Manning as copilot and Noonan as navigator, the Electra taxied down the runway. A slight crosswind made the plane drift slightly, and one wing dipped. As the plane pulled to the right, Amelia pulled the left throttle all the way back. Mantz, who was watching at the ramp, called out "Don't jockey those throttles" and watched helplessly as the wing hit the ground. The right landing gear was wrenched loose, gasoline sprayed, sparks flew, and the plane spun around. Amelia cut the ignition quickly, which prevented a fire, and the three fliers shakily climbed out. No one was hurt, but the Electra's right wing was almost totally destroyed, and the right wheel was torn off. The propellers, landing gear, and vertical stabilizer were also damaged.

When Mantz reached the plane, Amelia's first words were, "I don't know what happened, Paul." Mantz put an arm around her and said, "That's all right, Amelia. So long as nobody was hurt. You just didn't listen to Papa, did you?" He had previously instructed her that the only course of action under such conditions was to idle the throttles.

Someone standing nearby said, "Of course, now you will give up the trip?" Amelia shook her head, "I think not." She left the runway and went to call her husband in Oakland. Putnam was relieved to hear from her, as he had been called by a reporter and told that the plane was in flames. Nevertheless, he had not lost faith in her mission. When a newsman told Amelia a few hours later that no doubt her husband was relieved that the flight wouldn't happen, she showed him a telegram that Putnam had sent. It read, SO LONG AS YOU AND THE BOYS ARE OK THE REST DOESN'T MATTER STOP AFTER ALL IT'S JUST ONE OF THOSE

THINGS STOP WHETHER YOU WANT TO CALL IT A DAY OR KEEP GOING LATER IS EQUALLY JAKE WITH ME.

Amelia certainly wanted to keep going, but to do so involved extensive replanning. As the plane would take at least two months to repair, the original plan to fly east to west was scrapped, because weather conditions would be very different in early summer and favored a west to east direction. Amelia and her crew went back to California, and while the plane was being repaired at Oakland began to work out all the details of a new route. Captain Manning, meanwhile, who had been on leave from his ship in order to make the flight, had to go back to it. Amelia decided to make the trip with Fred Noonan only. It would be necessary for him to be with her for the entire trip, since the most difficult part, which was from Lae, New Guinea, to Howland Island, would now come at the end of the flight. Amelia had finally taken the advice of Bradford Washburn, and Putnam had made arrangements to have a Coast Guard cutter stationed at Howland so that she could make contact by radio. He had also reworked all diplomatic details and gasoline and parts accessibility and had raised another $50,000. In addition, money came in from such friends as the Odlums, Richard Byrd, and financier Bernard Baruch, and the mechanics who did the repairs accepted no fees out of admiration for Amelia.

When the repairs on the Electra were finally completed, Amelia decided to fly it from Oakland to Miami as a final "shakedown" and then begin the world flight from Miami. On May 22, Amelia, Putnam, Noonan, and Amelia's mechanic, Bo McKneely, took off for Miami and a week of final preparations. During this week, Amelia earned the admiration of the Pan Am mechanics, who were putting the finishing touches on the Electra, by pitching in whenever necessary and by the quiet, competent way she conducted herself. Although one of the most famous persons in the world, she had no problem in joining them for a simple lunch at the "greasy spoon" restaurant across the street from the airport. The mechanics had at first teased Fred Noonan, whom they had known from years before, about the flight. "Poor old Fred," they said, "flying around the world with a woman pilot." The more they got to know Amelia, however, the fewer teasing remarks they made. "Amelia is a grand person for such a trip," Noonan wrote to his new wife, whom he had married in Hawaii in March after the first flight failed. "She is the only woman flier I would care to make such an expedition with. Because in addition to being a fine companion and pilot, she can take hardships as well as a man—and work like one."

Amelia herself was determined that this should be her last record flight. She told reporter Carl Allen that she was "getting old," and that she wanted "to make way for the younger generation before I'm feeble, too." Her husband, who was beginning to have second thoughts about her making the trip, asked her that week in Miami if it was really necessary for her to go. She told him, "I've weighed it all carefully. With it behind me, life will be fuller and richer. I can be content. Afterwards, it will be fun to grow old." On June 1, 1937, a little less than two months before her fortieth birthday, Amelia said good-bye to George, and she and Fred climbed into the cockpit of the Electra and were off.

For the next thirty-two days, the two fliers went from Miami to San Juan, Puerto Rico; Caripito, Venezuela; Paramaribo, Dutch Guiana (now Surinam); Fortaleza, Brazil; Natal, Brazil; across the South Atlantic to Senegal, Mali, Chad, the Sudan, Ethiopia, Pakistan, India, Burma, Thailand, Singapore, Java, Timor Island near Bali, Australia, and New Guinea. Through it all, Amelia kept a diary about the different cultures through which they were quickly passing. At every stop along the way, no matter how brief her stay, she made an attempt to get at least a cursory look at the natives and made notes about their physical ap-

THE AROUND THE WORLD FLIGHT

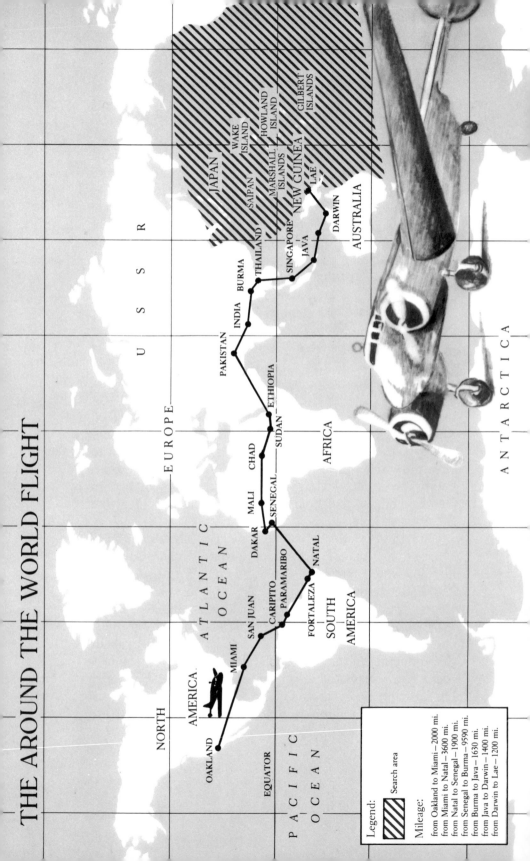

NORTH AMERICA.

EUROPE

U S S R

JAPAN

WAKE ISLAND

SAIPAN

MARSHALL ISLANDS

HOWLAND ISLAND

GILBERT ISLANDS

NEW GUINEA

LAE

DARWIN

AUSTRALIA

THAILAND

BURMA

INDIA

PAKISTAN

ETHIOPIA

SUDAN

CHAD

MALI

SENEGAL

DAKAR

AFRICA

SINGAPORE

JAVA

ATLANTIC OCEAN

NATAL

FORTALEZA

PARAMARIBO

CARIPITO

SAN JUAN

MIAMI

OAKLAND

SOUTH AMERICA

EQUATOR

PACIFIC OCEAN

ANTARCTICA

Legend:

Search area

Mileage:

from Oakland to Miami—2000 mi.
from Miami to Natal—3600 mi.
from Natal to Senegal—1900 mi.
from Senegal to Burma—9590 mi.
from Burma to Java—1630 mi.
from Java to Darwin—1400 mi.
from Darwin to Lae—1200 mi.

pearance and the way they lived. She also tried whenever possible to get away and see a bit of the country, once even riding a camel in India to do so. Africa particularly fascinated her, and in her diary she wrote:

When I was a little girl in Kansas, the adventures of travel fascinated me. With my sister and my cousins I gratified my ambitions by make-believe. That was in a barn behind our house in Atchison. There, in an old abandoned carriage, we made imaginary journeys full of fabulous perils.

Early we discovered the special joys of geography. The maps of far places that fell into our clutches supplemented the hair-raising experiences of the decrepit carriage. Map-traveling took its place beside window-shopping as an accepted diversion. The map of Africa was my favorite. The very word meant mystery. Blithely we rolled on our tongues such names as Senegal, Timbuctu, Ngami, El Fasher, and Khartoum. We weighed the advantages of the River Niger and Nile, the comparative ferociousness of the Tauregs and Swahili. No Livingstone, Stanley or Rhodes explored with more enthusiasm than we.

As the girl grew older, the inclination did not mend. Indeed, as flying brought far places closer, the horizon, and what lay beyond it, gained added lure.

More than once the Electra's pilot, who had been that little girl, thought of those early flights of fancy in the old carriage as she herself flew almost straight across Central Africa from the Atlantic to the Red Sea. For me the dreams of long ago had come true. Only, back in Atchison, our imaginary African treks were on camels or elephants. Then airplanes were of another day.

Putnam wanted Amelia back before the Fourth of July. More lectures, appearances, festivities, and a book contract awaited. Several times weather delayed the flight, and the pressure to hurry home mounted. "Push through," Amelia wrote in her diary, "we're always pushing through, hurrying on our long way, trying to get to some other place instead of enjoying the place we'd already got to. . . . Sometime I hope to stay somewhere as long as I like."

On July 2, Amelia and Fred left Lae, New Guinea, for the most difficult part of their trip—the 2,500-mile (4,000-km) flight over the Pacific to Howland Island. The month-long trip had taken its toll. Both were exhausted and ready to be home. They had repacked the plane, eliminating as much of their already scarce personal belongings as possible in order to save weight for the additional gas they would need to bring on board. The last words of Amelia's diary expressed her longing for the flight to be over:

Not much more than a month ago I was on the other shore of the Pacific, looking westward. This evening, I looked eastward over the Pacific. In those fast-moving days which have intervened, the whole width of the world has passed behind us—except this broad ocean. I shall be glad when we have the hazards of its navigation behind us.

An hour after taking off and again four hours later, Earhart contacted Lae on her day frequency. Three hours and twenty minutes later, she informed Lae that she was changing to her night frequency. Lae advised her not to change, as she was still coming in clearly. Probably she did not take that advice, because Lae did not hear from her again, and Amelia had no more two-way radio communication. The Coast Guard cutter *Ontario*, stationed midway between Lae and Howland, neither saw her nor had any communication with her. The cutter *Itasca* waited at Howland. Amelia was expected to reach the island about eighteen hours after takeoff. When she had been in the air about fourteen hours, Amelia's voice finally came in over the *Itasca* radio.

"Cloudy weather cloudy." The men in the radio room waited another hour before the voice came in again.

"*Itasca* from Earhart. *Itasca* broadcast on 3105 kilocycles on hour and half hour—repeat—broadcast on 3105 kilocycles on hour and half hour. Overcast."

The *Itasca* asked for her position, but she did not respond. Voice signals came in an hour later but were totally unreadable. For the next several hours, her voice would come in occasionally, but she never gave her position or stayed on long enough for the *Itasca* to get a bearing. She also kept switching frequencies, which confused matters still further. Finally, when she had been airborne for almost twenty-one hours, her voice, sounding strained, came through one last time: "We are on the line of position 157–337. Will repeat this message on 6210 kilocycles. Wait. Listening on 6210. We are running north and south."

The crew kept waiting, but nothing further was heard.

11

The men in the radio room of the *Itasca* were convinced by 10:00 A.M. that wherever the Electra was, her fuel would be running low. At 10:15, an hour and a half after Amelia's last radio message, the *Itasca* lifted anchor and started northwest toward the Gilbert Islands. There was little to go on except that Amelia had given her position as "157–337," and 337 indicated a northwest quadrant. The *Itasca* continued to transmit messages to the Electra, in case the plane was down but still afloat. Commander Thompson had radioed the news back to the mainland, and what would become the largest sea search in the history of the U.S. Navy was begun.

President Roosevelt authorized the Navy to use all available men, ships, and planes to search the 250,000 square miles (647,500 sq km) of Pacific in which the Electra might be located. The *Itasca* was joined by the aircraft carrier *Lexington,* which had been in Santa Barbara preparing for a July 4 celebration. The carrier's sixty planes were launched and covered 151,556 square miles (392,530 sq km) in five days. In addition the battleship *Colorado,* the minesweeper *Swan,* three destroyers, and many other vessels joined the search.

Congress protested to President Roosevelt that the

Navy was spending a quarter of a million dollars a day on the quest, but Roosevelt answered that the ships and planes were required to spend a certain amount of practice time in the sea and in the air, and such time should at least be for some real purpose. Of course, he was personally interested in the outcome of the search; he and his wife were close friends of Amelia.

George Putnam, too, had been notified immediately in San Francisco, where he had been waiting at the Coast Guard station. He quickly sent a radiogram to the naval search headquarters, located in Pearl Harbor, Honolulu: "If they are down, they can stay afloat indefinitely. Their empty tanks will give them buoyancy. Besides, they have all the emergency equipment they'll need—everything." He was comforted by the fact that the plane contained a life raft and food supplies. Remembering Jacqueline Cochran's successes with extrasensory perception, he immediately went to her Los Angeles apartment and begged for her help in locating Amelia. She later wrote in her book *The Stars at Noon:*

I told him where Amelia had gone down; that with the ditching of the plane Mr. Noonan, the navigator, had fractured his skull against the bulkhead in the navigator's compartment and was unconscious; but that Amelia was alive and the plane was floating in a certain area. I named a boat called the Itasca *which I had never heard of at the time as a boat that was nearby, and I also named another Japanese fighting vessel in that area, the name of which I now forget. I begged Putnam to keep my name out of it all but to get ships and planes out to the designated area. Navy planes and ships in abundance combed that area but found no trace.*

In the meantime, Putnam also contacted Mrs. Earhart in Los Angeles, where she was now living with him and Amelia, and gave her the news. When reporters arrived at her home, she met them composedly. When asked if she thought Amelia was dead, she said, "No, no, no! No, of course not. I know she's all right. I know she will soon be found. I know she is alive." In spite of the anxiety she must have been feeling, she responded personally to many of the hundreds of messages that began arriving daily.

As the days passed, the country could think of little else. The Earhart disappearance became one of the ten most reported news stories of the century. Newspapers and the radio tried to keep Americans abreast of both the disappearance and the search. Amateur radio operators from all over the country began claiming that they were receiving distress signals from Amelia, and George Putnam became a target for every psychic, crank, and practical joker who said that he knew where Amelia had gone down.

After two weeks and no trace of the Electra or its crew, the Navy and Coast Guard ordered their vessels to stop searching. When the *Lexington* returned to the San Francisco Harbor and passed under the Golden Gate Bridge, it lowered its colors to half-mast. Amelia and Fred Noonan were officially listed as "lost at sea."

For those closest to her, Amelia's disappearance was shattering, but each person managed to go on. Although George Putnam remarried just eighteen months after the disappearance, he continued to check out every possibility that might have led to finding Amelia. When he became a major in the Air Force during World War II and was stationed in the China-Burma-India theater, he continued to look for her. He divorced his new wife in 1944 and married again. After the war, he purchased the Stove Pipe Wells Hotel in Death Valley, California. Until his death in 1950, he continued his support and encouragement of the countless memorials to Amelia and her achievements. He saw that the diaries of her last flight, which she had mailed back to him at each stopping point on her trip, were published, and wrote his own biography of her, entitled *Soaring Wings*.

Amy Earhart endured her loss of Amelia for some years by maintaining her faith that her daughter would be found and rescued someday. For two years a suitcase containing clothing, sunburn cream, and scissors to cut Amelia's hair was kept packed and ready in case word came that she had been found. In 1953 Amy stated her belief that Amelia had been on a government mission and had been captured by the Japanese and been taken to Tokyo, where she had been killed. By this time, however, Amy was in her eighties, and her faculties were not what they had been. She was at that time living with Muriel and Albert in Medford, Massachusetts, and remained with them until her death in 1962.

Although Muriel hoped, like everyone else, that Amelia would someday return, she wrote less than a year after the disappearance that it seemed "better to face the situation and yield." Believing that "the plane must have crashed at once, and quickly and mercifully the water closed," she turned back to her family, her teaching, and her life in Medford, where she still lives. In 1963 she published her own book on her sister, *Courage Is the Price*, and has appeared at many functions honoring her sister's memory. Now in her eighties, she continues to be an invaluable source of information about Amelia, whether she is speaking to other biographers or to sixth-grade students in Medford.

It is fortunate that such a source of information exists, for the questions never end. In particular, Amelia's disappearance has created a mystery in which it seems everyone is interested. Almost from the moment the plane was lost various theories were formed that have refused to die. Hollywood even got into the act, producing in 1943 a film entitled *Flight for Freedom*, starring Rosalind Russell and Fred MacMurray. In the film, a famous American flier, "Tonie Carter," is asked by the government to go into hiding on a Pacific island so that the Navy, while supposedly looking for her, can get a look at Japanese installations. In the film, the plan is discovered, and rather than let the Japanese capture her, Tonie crashes her plane into the ocean. One subplot of the film was particularly infuriating to George Putnam. In it, the copilot was an old boyfriend of Tonie's. This gave rise to rumors that Amelia and Fred had engineered their disappearance so as to be able to go off together and live on a Pacific island. Putnam filed suit against the insinuations in the movie, and the film company settled out of court.

A scenario similar to the film's, however, was proposed by Joe Klaas and Joe Gervais in their 1970 book, *Amelia Earhart Lives*. Gervais believed that the plan was for Amelia to fly over Truk and the Marshalls, then to land on Canton Island and stay hidden so the Navy could search the Japanese islands. Supposedly there was a foul-up and Amelia was captured, sent to Japan, and imprisoned during World War II in the Imperial Palace in Tokyo. After the war, she was supposedly released on the condition that the emperor of Japan would not be tried as a war criminal and would remain head of state. Gervais and Klaas claimed to have found both Amelia and Noonan living under assumed names in the United States, although both individuals denied the theory.

The spy theory, however, persists. In the course of Fred Goerner's persistent odyssey discussed in Chapter 1, he learned that engines capable of greater speed than those on the Electra were installed on the plane. The purpose of this, he believes, was to allow Amelia and Noonan to make a side trip to Truk and survey the Japanese fleet base there. Having done this, Goerner says, she probably tried to fly on to Howland, got lost, and came down on what she thought was one of the British-held Gilbert Islands, but in fact was Mili Atoll, one of the Japanese-held Marshall Islands. As the Navy was not allowed into these islands, it was powerless to find her, or to prevent her capture, removal to Saipan, or death. In the course of his investigation, Goerner spoke to many who claimed to have seen Amelia during her capture and imprisonment. He also encountered enormous evasiveness by the military and the government during his investigation, and although he requested a congressional investigation to finally answer the questions to the mystery, one was never begun.

Thomas E. Devine, another investigator, also believed that the government was hiding something. He had been a technical sergeant on Saipan in 1944 and claimed to have seen the Electra there. He also said that natives had told him that a white man and woman, who had dropped from the sky, were buried in a cemetery there. Devine claimed that the U.S. government interfered with his investigation and that certain documents about Amelia had disappeared. Devine differed from Goerner, however, in that he believed that when the fliers could not find Howland, they tried to find Guam, the nearest U.S. territory, and in doing so actually landed on Saipan.

Yet another group of explorers found parts of an airplane in a canyon in Saipan in the late 1960s that they believed to be the Electra. They also interviewed several persons who said they had seen Amelia and Noonan. Bones found in a nearby cemetery were later determined to be of a Caucasian man and woman. When the group asked for help from the State Department, the department supposedly admitted to having a file on Amelia, but did not produce it. Meanwhile, servicemen who had been in the Marshalls after the 1944 invasion by the United States came forward with stories told to them by natives of a white man and woman who were pilots and had been captured by the Japanese.

As late as the summer of 1985, a book was published by Vincent V. Loomis, a former U.S. Air Force officer, with the help of a writer named Jeffrey L. Ethell. Loomis had been the operations officer on Eniwetok, Marshall Islands, during the first H-bomb test in the early 1950s. During this period, while he was helping to place colored marker panels on various islands to aid the pilots in their tests, he discovered an airplane on an atoll. Years later, after reading about

Fred Goerner's search, he began his own. After many inquiries and six expeditions to the Pacific and Japan, he concluded that the fliers' departure from Lae, New Guinea, at 10:00 A.M. meant that they flew over Japanese-mandated territory in the middle of the night, making surveillance impossible. He also pointed to the lack of intelligence-gathering equipment and Amelia's pacifism as making the spy theory unlikely. He believes that Amelia and Noonan simply flew off course by mistake, but agrees with Goerner and Devine that they were captured and taken to Saipan, where he believes Noonan was executed and Amelia died of dysentery.

Despite all the theories that have come down through the years, the real importance of Amelia Earhart does not lie with her disappearance, a mystery that only serves to enhance a legend that would have existed in any case. Although she was never the most technically proficient of pilots, her courage enabled her to succeed at making the most challenging and hazardous flights of her time, and to capture the attention of the world. Because she and others like her pioneered the cause, aviation is now a technology that we accept as an integral part of our everyday lives. An intense pacifist, Amelia believed that knowing other cultures was a first step toward preventing conflict. Fascinated by the differences she saw among peoples all over the world, she wanted everyone to have the same chance to see these differences, and she saw aviation as a force that could "shrink" the globe. As aviation entered the Jet Age, it could look to her and to others like her as the visionaries of modern travel.

Amelia's achievements do not end there, however. Women everywhere have looked to her as a symbol of what can be achieved by a woman if only she dares to realize her full potential. As more and more women have begun to lead independent lives and careers, many feel an enormous debt of thanks to her who was one of the first to do so. Her courage and vision have not influenced women only, however; she has provided inspiration to both sexes. Several days after her disappearance, Walter Lippmann wrote in his daily column:

The world is a better place to live in because it contains human beings who will give up ease and security, and stake their own lives in order to do what they themselves think worth doing . . .

In such persons mankind overcomes the inertia which would keep it earthbound forever in its habitual ways. They have in them the free and useless energy with which alone men surpass themselves . . .

They do the useless, brave, noble, the divinely foolish and the very wisest things that are done by men. And what they prove to themselves and to others is that man is no mere creature of his habits, no mere automaton in his routine, no mere cog in the collective machine, but that in the dust of which he is made there is also fire, lighted now and then by great winds from the sky.

COURAGE

Courage is the price that life exacts for granting peace.

The soul that knows it not, knows no release
From little things;

Knows not the livid loneliness of fear
Nor mountain heights, where bitter joy can hear
The sound of wings.

How can life grant us boon of living, compensate
For dull grey ugliness and pregnant hate
Unless we dare

The soul's dominion? Each time we make a choice, we pay
With courage to behold resistless day
And count it fair.

Amelia Earhart

BIBLIOGRAPHY

SOURCES

Backus, Jean L. *Letters from Amelia.* Boston: Beacon Press, 1982.

Briand, Paul L., Jr. *Daughter of the Sky.* New York: Duell, Sloan and Pearce, 1960.

Burke, John. *Winged Legend.* New York: G. P. Putnam's Sons, 1970.

Cochran, Jacqueline. *The Stars at Noon.* Boston: Little, Brown, 1954.

Earhart, Amelia. *Last Flight.* New York: Harcourt, Brace, and World, 1937.

——————. *The Fun of It.* New York: Harcourt, Brace, and World, 1932.

——————. *20 Hrs., 40 Mins.* New York: G. P. Putnam's Sons, 1928.

Goerner, Fred. *The Search for Amelia Earhart.* New York: Doubleday, 1966.

Klaas, Joe. *Amelia Earhart Lives.* New York: McGraw-Hill, 1970.

Lindbergh, Anne Morrow. *Hour of Gold, Hour of Lead.* New York: Harcourt, Brace Jovanovich, 1973.

Loomis, Vincent V. and Jeffry L. Ethell. *Amelia Earhart: The Final Story*. New York: Random House, 1985.

Moolman, Valerie, and eds. *Women Aloft*. Alexandria, Virginia: Time-Life Books, 1981.

Morrissey, Muriel Earhart. *Courage Is the Price*. Wichita, Kansas: McCormick-Armstrong Publishing Division, 1963.

Prendergast, Curtis. *The First Aviators*. Alexandria, Virginia: Time-Life Books, 1981.

Putnam, George Palmer. *Soaring Wings*. New York: Harcourt, Brace, and Company, 1939.

Railey, Hilton H. *Touch'd with Madness*. New York: Carrick and Evans, 1938.

The author is also most grateful for the time and patience of Muriel Earhart Morrissey.

SUGGESTIONS FOR
FURTHER READING

Bowen, Ezra, and eds. *Knights of the Air*. Alexandria, Virginia: Time-Life Books, 1980.

Brooks-Pazmany, Kathleen. *United States Women in Aviation 1919–1929*. Washington: Smithsonian Institution Press, 1983.

Lindbergh, Charles A. *The Spirit of St. Louis*. New York: Charles Scribner's Sons, 1953.

Lindbergh, Charles A. *We*. New York: G. P. Putnam's Sons, 1927.

O'Neil, Paul. *Barnstormers and Speed Kings*. Alexandria, Virginia: Time-Life Books, 1981.

Planck, Charles E. *Women with Wings*. New York: Harper & Brothers, 1942.

RECORDS

SET BY
AMELIA EARHART

Altitude of 14,000 feet, Long Beach, California, October 1922.

First woman to cross the Atlantic by air, June 1928.

First woman to solo on transcontinental roundtrip, September 1928.

Speed record for women, Los Angeles, California, November 1929.

Speed record for 100 km, Detroit, Michigan, June 1930.

Broke altitude record for autogiros at 15,000 feet and then broke own record by going to 18,415 feet on same day, Willow Grove, Pennsylvania, April 1931.

First woman to solo Atlantic and first person to cross Atlantic by air twice, May 1932.

Women's nonstop transcontinental speed record, Los Angeles, California, to Newark, New Jersey, August 1932.

Broke own 1931 transcontinental speed record, July 1933.

First person to fiy Hawaii to California, first person to solo anywhere in the Pacific, and first person to solo over both Atlantic and Pacific oceans, January 1935.

First person to solo from Los Angeles, California, to Mexico City, Mexico, April 1935.

First person to solo from Mexico to Newark, New Jersey, May 1935.

Record for east to west crossing, Oakland, California, to Honolulu, Hawaii, March 1937.

Around the world at the equator, June–July, 1937 (not completed)

INDEX